The Language of Localization

Katherine Brown-Hoekstra

The Content Wrangler
Content Strategy Series

The Language of Localization

Credits

Series Producer:	Scott Abel
Copy Editor:	Trey DeGrassi
Indexer:	Cheryl Landes
Series Cover Designer:	Marc Posch
Publishing Advisor:	Don Day
Publisher:	Richard Hamilton

Permissions

The definition of the term Internationalization Tag Set is derived from the W3C recommendation: Internationalization Tag Set (ITS) Version 2.0, Copyright © 2013 W3C, (MIT, ERCIM, Keio, Beihang). http://www.w3.org/Consortium/Legal/2015/doc-license

Disclaimer

Trademarks

XML Press
Laguna Hills, California
http://xmlpress.net

First Edition
ISBN: 978-1-937434-58-8 (print)
ISBN: 978-1-937434-59-5 (ebook)

Table of Contents

Foreword

Like many of you, I have frequently had to explain what localization is, usually in the context of what I do for a living. I find localization easy to explain, often using the example of getting a mobile phone adapted for other countries. Because most people own one, they can imagine why adaptation makes sense. For good measure, I add that it is not only the language, but often local laws, different technical specifications, and customs that need to be considered.

As I get fired up and start explaining the difference between localization and internationalization, eyes quickly glaze over because, like in all languages, words are not just words; they represent concepts that, in turn, often rely on the comprehension of other concepts for a clear understanding. At this point, the value of a guide like *The Language of Localization* becomes apparent. Like any other profession, we have developed a language of our own. We took common words that have multiple meanings and defined them in the context of localization, or if a word did not exist, we invented one.

This sounds a lot easier than it is because there is no central authority to do that work, no arbiter to clarify meaning. Instead, it was, and continues to be, a crowd-sourced exercise with no central repository to use for reference.

Enter Kit Hoekstra-Brown, Scott Abel, Richard Hamilton, and their merry band of subject matter experts. For the benefit of localization professionals, global marketers, and technical communicators, they compiled a "must-know" list of terms that define the common language of our industry.

I appreciate how thoroughly they tackled the task. Not only are the terms defined clearly and their importance explained, but in the essay, they explain why business professionals need to have this information.

Which brings to mind a case when poor communication and a lack of clearly defined terms cost a pretty penny. In 1999, NASA lost a US$125 million Mars orbiter because NASA was using metric measurements, while Lockheed Martin, the contractor, relied on English Imperial units.[1].

---

[1] Grossman, Lisa. *Wired* magazine. "Metric Math Mistake Muffed Mars Meteorology Mission." https://tlolink.com/2xBXppE

We can do better. Having clarity in the way we communicate about the many tasks and processes that make up life in localization benefits every aspect of our work. It helps us achieve good quality, speeds up time to market, and improves the cost effectiveness of our collaboration. Everyone benefits, from the translator to the project managers to, maybe most important of all, the end users.

We all owe thanks to the people behind this project for helping to develop a shared language for a still young industry. Along with other standards, it is a critical tool in meeting the challenges of an ever faster-paced, globalized world.

As new terms appear and existing ones change their meaning, I hope that the authors will issue new editions of this excellent guide.

Well done, and thank you on behalf of the whole localization community.

Ulrich Henes
Madison, Wisconsin, USA

About Ulrich Henes

Ulrich Henes is the founder and president of The Localization Institute, a Madison Wisconsin-based consulting and event organizing company, and is co-producer of the LocWorld conferences. From his earliest years, Ulrich has been fascinated by language, cultural differences, and global business. He spent the first decade of his career organizing international campaigns against the arms race and apartheid and promoting global social justice. For the past 25 years Ulrich has channeled his passion for all things global into promoting awareness and respect for differences among people, countries, and languages in the international business community.

Preface

> "Knowledge is power. Information is liberating. Education is the premise of progress, in every society, in every family."
>
> —Kofi Annan

The *Language of...* series is the brainchild of Scott Abel and Rahel Anne Bailie, beginning with *The Language of Content Strategy*. This book, *The Language of Localization*, is the 3rd book in the series and gathers experts from around the world to discuss core concepts in localization.

Over the next year, we will highlight a term each week on our website: http://thelanguageoflocalization.com. This book is meant to open the conversation around the terminology we use and help clients and new professionals develop a better understanding of our industry.

As someone once said, localization is the biggest industry that no one has ever heard of. Perhaps, that is because localization is part of the infrastructure that keeps the global economy ticking along. We touch every product, process, and service on this planet and off of it, and our work often goes unnoticed until something goes wrong.

Because this industry is both broad and deep, it was challenging to pare the terminology in this book down to 52 terms, and we made adjustments along the way as our expert contributors weighed in. Those of you who have read the other books in the series will notice that some of the terms are familiar. Where possible, we practiced what we preach and reused the topics from the other books in the series, making changes where needed to appeal to this audience.

We also added three appendices of tangentially related terms that are important to localization. And, you might notice that the numbered references are not in numerical order in the text. This is because, in some cases, references are used by multiple authors, and so are listed under the topic in which they first appear.

The best part of this project was working with colleagues from all over the world who generously shared their knowledge. Their expertise and willingness to add to the body of knowledge are the heart of this book.

It is my hope that this book, and others like it, will raise the profile of our profession and help make the black box of localization a bit more transparent to our clients and to those who are just starting in the profession.

Acknowledgments

It is such a privilege to work with talented people from all over the globe. This project would not have been possible without the work and care of many experts in the localization industry. To my friends and colleagues who contributed their knowledge to this project, I thank you. You have advanced our profession with your work.

The Language of... series is the brainchild of Scott Abel and Rahel Anne Bailie, and published by XML Press. Richard Hamilton, Don Day, Scott Abel, and Trey DeGrassi were instrumental in keeping the project on track and providing encouragement and advice.

I would also like to thank Donna Parrish, Ulrich Henes, Arle Lommel, David Filip, Dave Ruane, Rick McGowan, and others who generously shared their networks to help me find contributors.

Richard Sikes and Arle Lommel magnanimously shared their expertise and suggestions on a couple of the more challenging topics. Arle Lommel and Madison Van Doren went the extra mile, both writing topics for the main text and using their specialized knowledge to create the standards and linguistics appendices, respectively.

Katherine (Kit) Brown-Hoekstra
October 2017

Core Concepts

Aljoscha Burchardt
Bitext

What is it?

A collection (usually electronic) of texts in two languages that can be considered translations of each other and that are aligned at the sentence or paragraph level.

Why is it important?

A bitext is one of the most basic results of translation. It can be used in the language industry for training, revision, and quality control. Bitexts also serve as training data for statistical *machine translation*.

About Aljoscha Burchardt

Aljoscha Burchardt is lab manager at the Language Technology Lab of the German Research Center for Artificial Intelligence (DFKI GmbH). He is an expert in artificial intelligence and language technology. His interests include the evaluation of (machine) translation quality and the inclusion of language professionals in the MT R&D workflow. Burchardt is co-developer of the MQM framework for measuring translation quality. He has a background in semantic language technology.

Email	aljoscha.burchardt@dfki.de
Website	dfki.de/~aburch/
Twitter	@albu
LinkedIn	linkedin.com/in/aljoschaburchardt/
Facebook	facebook.com/aljoscha.burchardt

Why does a business professional need to know this?

In linguistics, a sentence is often considered as a natural unit. In translation, a translated sentence pair is, therefore, also a natural unit.

From a technical point, bitexts are a straightforward representation of the source text and the product of translation[3]. They can serve as an exchange or interface format between localization experts, system developers, and machines. Bitexts play a key role in training, evaluating, and improving localization technologies, such as *translation memories*, terminology management tools, or machine translation engines. They can also serve as a basic format for proofreading and interaction with customers, e.g., in the process of formal quality control. *XLIFF* is a standard format for representing bitexts in localization processes.

If bitexts are used for training language technology applications, they must provide the application with all information necessary for their intended functionality. To do this, they need to have optimal quality, represent a sensible range of linguistic variation, and have a large enough vocabulary. In general, it is best to use bitexts based on literal, uncreative translations when setting up translation engines.

Bitexts usually present (complete) ordered texts that are normally aligned at the sentence or paragraph level[4]. This makes it possible to study the meaning of larger linguistic texts, also known as discourse, such as how texts organize information, are coherent, and reference topics both inside and outside of the current text. Such analyses can be used to improve the quality of the translation memory and, in the case of machine translation, to train the system.

Katherine (Kit) Brown-Hoekstra
Culture

What is it?
The sum total of worldview, expectations, manners, activities, traditions, language, dress, and belief systems, including thoughts, feelings, and actions that distinguish one group from another.

Why is it important?
Culture provides a reference point, with cultural differences and assumptions often fueling conflict. More positively, culture also connects people and sets a society's rhythm of life.

About Katherine (Kit) Brown-Hoekstra
Katherine (Kit) Brown-Hoekstra is a Fellow of the Society for Technical Communication (STC), former STC Society President, and a member of the Colorado State University Media Hall of Fame. She is an experienced consultant with over 25 years of experience in technical communication and localization.

As Principal of Comgenesis, LLC, Kit provides consulting and training to her clients on a variety of topics, including localization, content strategy, and content management. She speaks at conferences worldwide and publishes regularly in industry magazines. Her blog is www.pangaeapapers.com.

Email	kit.brown@comgenesis.com
Website	comgenesis.com
Twitter	@kitcomgenesis
LinkedIn	linkedin.com/pub/kit-brown-hoekstra/0/321/71b

Why does a business professional need to know this?

Geert Hofstede calls culture "the collective programming of the mind that distinguishes the members of one group or category of people from others." [19]. Culture is learned and dynamic, and it provides the framework upon which human beings relate to each other and their world. Culture occurs at multiple levels, from geographic to linguistic, from governmental to familial, from societal to corporate, and so on.

These multiple levels of culture provide context for interpreting experiences by identifying the environment and value system in effect for the participants when interaction or communication occurs[18]. This context dictates the narrative and outcome, as well as the emphasis, emotion, metaphor and word play, and level of optimism expressed by the author. Because different cultures admire and focus on different attributes or aspects of the environment, understanding the context provided by a culture is key to successfully reaching customers where they live and work.

Cultural context is particularly important with marketing and branding messages because these types of communication often depend on shared understanding of cultural nuances to be successful. Plays on words are particularly challenging to localize. Even something as simple as using a graphic with a check mark (aka a tick mark) and an envelope for *check for new e-mail* only works in English because the word for *check mark* and the verb *to check* are not the same in other languages:

- French = marque dc coche vs. vérifier
- Spanish = marca de verificación vs. comprobar
- Italian = segno di spunta vs. controlla la posta

Catherine Deschamps-Potter
Fluency

What is it?

The ability to speak or write a foreign language easily and accurately and to comprehend most communication.

Why is it important?

Fluency enables the user of a language to focus on making connections among ideas. By making connections, the reader can focus his/her attention on comprehension. For most languages, fluency means having a minimum of 15,000 to 20,000 words in your vocabulary and being able to use them correctly in context[32].

About Catherine Deschamps-Potter

Catherine Deschamps-Potter is VP of Sales and Marketing at ICD Translation. She has been in the localization industry for over 25 years and has built the core of ICD's client base through a deep understanding of individual client's needs. Her natural professionalism is reinforced yearly by the number of clients returning to ICD Translation and the partnerships they have developed with ICD Translation.

Email	catherine@icdtranslation.com
Website	icdtranslation.com
LinkedIn	linkedin.com/in/catherine-deschamps-potter-4a90943
Facebook	facebook.com/catherine.deschampspotter

Why does a business professional need to know this?

In the localization industry, fluency is a key concept. It goes far beyond the basic definition of listening, speaking, reading, and writing. Fluency includes understanding the intricacies of language and cultural nuances, as well as mastering expressions, colloquialisms, and even onomatopoeia[31]. Clients expect their translations to relay the same ideas as the original source content. Language professionals must not only constantly work to remain expert in both the source and target languages, they must be fluent in the industry they specialize in.

Cultural fluency is key to global customers. It takes more than physical expansion and translated documents to satisfy global clients. The one-size-fits-all approach does not work with global customers, and many large corporations have paid dearly for failing in this area.

With a clear insight into those markets, as well as deep knowledge of consumer preferences, localization vendors can help clients avoid such mistakes. A customized approach feels real and authentic to consumers. Companies can then increase customer engagement on global websites, build trust, and expand brand awareness.

It is crucial to think like the customer and to be culturally fluent to secure revenue growth. Business professionals doing business internationally have to be culturally fluent to work together effectively.

Anna Schlegel
Globalization (g11n)

What is it?

The art and science of analyzing, planning, and aligning the corporate strategies, product design, content, marketing, packaging, and support materials required to support a business in all its markets worldwide.

Why is it important?

Globalization allows companies to increase their reach by skillfully guiding the process of taking a product, service, idea, system, and project to multiple markets. It must be an integral part of the corporate strategy to enable growth in global markets and to effectively reach global audiences.

About Anna Schlegel

Anna Schlegel is Sr. Director of Information Engineering & Globalization at NetApp, ensuring that the right content reaches the right people, when, where, and how they need it, in the language they prefer: their own. She has led globalization teams for 20+ years with large enterprises and for two localization vendors as the CEO and general manager. Anna speaks regularly at universities, corporations, and other international organizations, authored *Truly Global, The Theory and Practice of Bringing Your Company to International Markets* [39], and has published articles on Forbes.com, Fortune.com, GALA-global.org, and Multilingual.com. She co-founded Women in Localization and chairs Women in Technology at NetApp. *The Diversity Journal* named her a 2017 Women Worth Watching in STEM Award.

Email	Anna.Schlegel@netapp.com
Twitter	@annapapallona
LinkedIn	linkedin.com/in/annanschlegel/

Why does a business professional need to know this?

Globalization requires much more than simply having an international office, developing local language websites, or preparing code for *localization*. It is an ongoing effort to remove barriers so that customers have a good experience, wherever they live and work.

At its best, globalization is built into the overall corporate strategy and infused into every area and activity in the company. This strategic focus goes hand in hand with *internationalization*, which is the technical side of globalization. The globalization strategy drives the priorities, budget, and focus for internationalization and, subsequently, for localization and translation.

In addition to encompassing internationalization and localization, globalization also includes global trade compliance, OEM partnerships, joint ventures, regulatory compliance, as well as your global content strategy.

For example, if you sell medical equipment, you must create products that comply with local medical regulations. By understanding these regulatory differences and removing barriers to purchasing and using a product or service in the local market, globalization teams can help you build market share.

To be successful, companies need the right leaders in place at all levels of the organization to take full advantage of the opportunities that globalization provides. These leaders must fully support globalization and have experience in incorporating best practices for globalization into all of the company's processes and systems, as well as an understanding of the needs and drivers for each of your markets[40].

An experienced globalization team can help you prioritize your efforts and help you capitalize on global opportunities[39].

Alison Toon
In-Country Review (ICR)

What is it?
A step in the content workflow, after translation and prior to publishing, where the content is reviewed by a person who is intimately familiar with the target audience – usually a person who lives and works for the client in the target market and often a person who is not a translator, for example, a member of the marketing team.

Why is it important?
The ICR finds final issues and is often the final approval before publishing. It can be a bottleneck in the localization process. Particularly in regulated industries, it is critical to have a local market expert review translated, localized, and *transcreated* content for correctness, quality, and appropriateness.

About Alison Toon
Alison Toon helps global enterprises to enable worldwide business by managing complex content, translation, and globalization strategies and by consulting on operations, business processes, and technologies. She helps the diverse and complex enterprise to speak with one voice, regardless of language: to think local, while acting global. And in her spare time, she photographs rock stars, writes children's books, researches family history, and manages one or two blogs.

Email	alisontoon00@gmail.com
Website	alisontoon.com
Twitter	@alisontoon
LinkedIn	linkedin.com/in/alisontoon
Facebook	facebook.com/alisontoon

Why does a business professional need to know this?

An important step in global content management, in-country reviews often provide final sign-off for translation quality. A good relationship among in-country reviewers, translators, and linguistic leads helps to speed the process, generate trust, and improve content quality. A trained reviewer knows what to look for, knows what should (and should not) be changed or reported as an error, and is the best person to help with terminology.

ICR can be a process bottleneck:

- Reviewers have other responsibilities and little time for ICR work.
- Reviews are subjective, and everyone has their own opinion.

Check that reviewers:

- Know what content to expect, when it will arrive, and what the deadlines are.
- Are trained on what to flag (misused terminology, non-brand voice) and what to ignore (I would have said it differently).
- Are involved in terminology identification and review.
- Are available and willing to participate.

You also need a backup plan in case a reviewer is unresponsive or becomes unavailable.

An ICR is a good health check of the end-to-end content process. If there are very few ICR issues, the content workflow might be perfect, or the reviewers might be overwhelmed. If reviewers flag many basic issues, such as typos, the translation and QA steps must be revised to prevent these issues from reaching ICR. If reviewers complain about translation quality but cannot pinpoint exact issues, and you are certain that the translation is good, then the problem may be more fundamental: the source content may be inappropriate for the target market, no matter how perfectly it is translated[56] [57] [58].

John Yunker
Internationalization (i18n)

What is it?

A process by which content – online, in print, in software, or in other types of media – is made world ready, so it can be localized with minimal rewriting, redesigning, or re-engineering.

Why is it important?

Helps organizations save significant time and resources by creating world-ready architecture and content before moving on to localization and translation.

About John Yunker

John Yunker, co-founder of Byte Level Research (www.bytelevel.com), consults with many of the world's leading global brands, providing web globalization training and benchmark services. He is author of *Think Outside the Country: A Guide to Going Global and Succeeding in the Translation Economy* [59] and the annual report, *The Web Globalization Report Card*. He blogs at www.GlobalbyDesign.com.

Email	jyunker@bytelevel.com
Website	bytelevel.com
Twitter	@johnyunker
LinkedIn	linkedin.com/in/johnyunker/

Why does a business professional need to know this?

Internationalization, sometimes abbreviated as i18n, is the first stage toward taking software, websites, and other content global. Before localizing anything, it's important to first take a step back and ask: Is it world ready?

Internationalizing text means creating a universal English source text in which sentences are optimized for translation. Edits can include removing culturally specific metaphors (for example, "A home run offer!"), removing humor (which rarely translates well), and keeping sentences short and declarative.

When designing websites or software, internationalization entails creating an architecture and design templates that can be supported across all locales with no engineering changes. Requirements can include support for the world's many scripts, currencies, date, measurement display formats, and address formats. The most efficient global templates often avoid embedding text within images because such images must be manually edited for each language supported.

Templates must be flexible enough to allow for text expansion – text strings often double in length when translating from English into languages such as Dutch, German, or Russian. Also, images and icons in global templates must be carefully reviewed to ensure they are globally relevant and usable.

In their rush to go global, companies often overlook internationalization. As a consequence, a website or app created for one locale often must be redesigned to support a different locale. Internationalization ensures that companies can avoid that extra work and go global more efficiently[59] [60].

Nataly Kelly
Interpreting

What is it?
The act of converting verbal (spoken or signed) communication from one language into another.

Why is it important?
Written translation and spoken or signed language interpreting are two very different, but related, professions. Localization specialists source solutions for diverse needs, usually for people who are not specialists in the fields of translation and interpreting. When a requesting party asks for translation services, they might actually need interpreting services instead. For example, a marketer organizing a company event might request translation for the CEO's presentation. A localization specialist might assume this means translation of written slides, but later finds out the person requesting the service actually needs spoken language interpreters. Because these requests are frequently confused, it's important to know how to handle them when they occur.

About Nataly Kelly
Nataly Kelly is a global business and localization leader who loves helping companies grow internationally. She is passionate about inbound marketing and is a fan of B2B SaaS. Nataly is co-author, with Jost Zetsche, of the book *Found in Translation: How Language Shapes Our Lives and Transforms the World* [65]. Nataly is a former translator and interpreter, Fulbright scholar in sociolinguistics, and lifelong language learner.

Email	nkelly@hubspot.com
Website	natalykelly.com
Twitter	@natalykelly
LinkedIn	linkedin.com/in/natalykelly/

Why does a business professional need to know this?

Within the field of interpreting, there are three types of interpreting services that businesses most frequently require:

- **Conference interpreting:** live interpreting of a presentation or a webinar, usually at a company's user conference or internally run event.
- **Escort interpreting:** a typical practice for business discussions or negotiations where the parties do not share a common language and, therefore, need an interpreter. This is quite common for dealings between Japan and Western countries, for example.
- **Remote interpreting:** used for shorter conversations, such as phone calls or video calls, in which parties do not share a common language and communicate through an interpreter who is in another location.

Each service has different types of service providers, is suited to different use cases, and has different billing methods.

Finding and hiring interpreters differs greatly from sourcing translation services. Conference and escort interpreters are usually booked directly in the country where they are needed, through a professional association such as AIIC.net[64], although they can be booked via agencies that work with AIIC interpreters and provide equipment rental. These services are usually booked for the day or, less commonly, by the half-day, with multiple interpreters being booked on a rotation to ensure that a fresh interpreter is continually available. Remote interpreting is billed by the minute and offered by telephone and video interpreting companies.

When businesses rely on their own bilingual employees as interpreters, this can create a high risk and opportunity cost. Professional services are more reliable, but interpreters should be briefed in detail in advance to provide optimal quality[65] [66].

Richard Sikes
Language Pair

What is it?

In localization, a language pair identifies the combination of one unique *source language* variant with one unique *target language* variant.

Why is it important?

Language pairs are a basic unit of translation. The source contains original content, which is then translated into a target language. The pairs are generally expressed with implied translation direction: source before target.

About Richard Sikes

Richard Sikes has been immersed in technical translation and localization for over 30 years. He is passionate about linguistic technologies of all kinds. Richard managed localization teams at several industry-leading software companies. He contributes frequently to *MultiLingual* magazine, and is well-known as a speaker at translation industry events. Richard holds a BA from the University of California, Diplom Betriebswirt (FH) from the Fachhochschule Heidelberg, and an MBA from the University of Toronto.

Email	richards@contentrules.com
Website	contentrules.com
Twitter	@locflowtech
LinkedIn	ca.linkedin.com/in/richardsikes

Why does a business professional need to know this?

The language pair designation provides clarity and facilitates granularity for planning and executing localization projects. If a project comprises more than one source or target language, then each source/target combination is an individual language pair. Typical examples include: English/German, Dutch/Afrikaans, or Simplified Chinese/French. A language pair could also consist of two variants of the same language, for example, European French/Canadian French[68] [69].

The relationship between the two members of a language pair is most frequently direct, but it can be indirect. For some language combinations, appropriate linguistic resources can be hard to find. In this case, a *pivot language* is used. The source language, for example Japanese, is translated first into a more universal language such as English, and from English into target languages. So, the Japanese-to-target language pair has been created, although the means for creating it is indirect. This method can cause some ambiguity in translation quality, but not necessarily. If indirect language pairs are reused (also called *leveraging*), then the localization team imposes a *matching penalty* because translations done this way tend to be less precise.

Translation service providers often possess greater linguistic or subject matter expertise in some language pairs than in others. Larger projects are sometimes split up between service providers, based on their relative strengths per language pair. To choose the right vendor, achieve optimal quality, and avoid confusion, costly rework, and project delay, a localization specialist must accurately specify the language-pair deliverables[67].

Patricia Doest
Leverage

What is it?

Leverage means re-using (parts of) a given text, both in content creation and content localization.

Why is it important?

The main goal for all localized content should be to achieve the highest quality, in the shortest time, at the lowest cost. Leverage can help make content more consistent. This increases the quality and makes localization efforts more cost-efficient.

About Patricia Doest

Patricia Doest is a global content expert with over 10 years' experience in the localization industry, both on the vendor and the buyer sides. As Manager of the Globalization department at Spil Games, she successfully set up a global content strategy, created visibility for localization, and transformed the department from an operational bottleneck into a well-oiled machine. Her mission is to break down barriers between buyers of language services and localization service providers (LSPs) by educating both sides in how to set common key performance indicators (KPIs) and communicate in a transparent way.

Email   patricia.doest@spilgames.com
LinkedIn   linkedin.com/in/patriciadoest/

Why does a business professional need to know this?

Leverage allows us to produce more consistent, higher quality content, while at the same time working faster and saving costs.

Segmenting the text as granularly as possible increases the opportunities for reuse. Usually, localization specialists keep track of the text segments in a *Translation Memory (TM)*, and match it with a target language. When translators use a *Computer Aided Translation (CAT)* tool, it enables them to store the TM and make sure they only translate a particular text segment once. When they find a similar – but not identical – text segment, the tool flags it as a *fuzzy match* and displays it in the CAT tool so the translator can evaluate the match.

On the content development side, the term leverage is often referred to as reuse, which means that the same or similar content is used in multiple places in the source content. This type of leverage also improves consistency in the source, as well as the target.

The benefit of leverage is seen in consistent translations and a decrease in cost for similar text. Often, the client views leverage as positive (we can save money), while the localization vendor views it as negative (I am getting paid for only a fraction of the work I do).

All stakeholders in the localization industry should embrace leverage: content developers, translators, localization project managers (vendor- and client-side), localization managers, and quality assurance specialists[70] [71].

Chris Raulf
Locale

What is it?
The combination of specific geographic location and the language, or dialect, spoken in that particular region.

Why is it important?
Understanding the locale concept is fundamental to succeeding with localization because you may need to create distinct content for two locales, even if the two use the same language. For example, German is the official language in both Germany and Austria. Yet, residents of these two locales frequently use different terms to describe the same thing.

About Chris Raulf
Chris Raulf is the founder of Boulder SEO Marketing, a Boulder and Denver-based digital marketing agency. The company assists global customers with all of their search engine optimization needs. Chris is an international keynote speaker and his online SEO training allows anyone to implement a powerful digital marketing strategy. His international background makes him one of the few professionals in the industry who truly live and breathe multilingual search engine optimization on a daily basis.

Email	chris@boulderseomarketing.com
Website	boulderseomarketing.com/
Twitter	@swisschris
LinkedIn	linkedin.com/in/chrisraulf/
Facebook	facebook.com/BoulderSEOMarketing

Why does a business professional need to know this?

Understanding and targeting a locale instead of a language is particularly important when it comes to website localization projects. Even when the same language is spoken in two locales, word choice and other cultural differences might exist.

Applying locale-specific *multilingual search engine optimization (MSEO)* best practices is especially crucial to the overall success of these projects. MSEO, the process of optimizing a website and content to rank prominently in search engines, could increase organic search traffic, generate more leads, and possibly increase sales[72].

If you simply target a language, it might not cover every area where that language is spoken. For example, the German-speaking population in Switzerland might use different nuances of the language than the German-speaking population in Germany.

As another example, let's say one of your English target SEO keywords is *cell phone* and you are targeting German-speaking customers in Germany and Switzerland. Using tools such as Google Global Market Finder and Google Keyword Planner, you see that people in Germany use the term *handy* instead of a literal translation of the term *cell phone*. You also see that most people in Germany use the term *handy,* while a small fraction of people use the term *natel*. However, in the German-speaking part of Switzerland, it is a nearly 50/50 split between *handy* and *natel*.

If you had focused only on *natel*, you would not have reached part of your target audience. In this example, you would definitely want to include both keywords in your strategy for Switzerland[73].

James V. Romano
Localization (l10n)

What is it?
Adaptation of content to make it more meaningful, appropriate, and effective for a particular culture, locale, or market.

Why is it important?
Localization increases the relevance of the content for a particular target audience by ensuring that it meets the needs of the local market. Localization is a US$40 billion industry and growing[74].

About James V. Romano
Ever since he was a small child trying to understand his Italian grandfather at the dinner table, James Romano has been trying to unravel the mysteries of languages and cultures. For 30 years now, his company, Prisma International, has been helping clients communicate with their global customers, audiences, and users.

Email   jromano@prisma.com
Website   prisma.com

Why does a business professional need to know this?

Localization, sometimes abbreviated as l10n, is an essential process in the content lifecycle. More than just an add-on at the end of the content development cycle, localization requires careful planning and strategy right from the start.

To be effective, content must be relevant and meaningful to the target audience. Localization is the process by which content is made more appropriate and more meaningful for a particular culture. Without localization, content developers would be spinning generic pablum in the hope that users (near or far) will recognize a scintilla of meaning, latch on, and perhaps buy the product, heed the warning, or swallow the pitch.

Localization is strategic: it requires a comprehensive, planned approach in which all parts of the content system – the messaging, technologies, and audience – come together in a dynamic, creative process, producing what can best be described as an *aha* moment. Localized content taps into the power of local culture and uses it to project and amplify its message to create a deeper, more resonant message.

Localization is about producing an *aha* in any language, culture, or medium. A content strategy that doesn't lead to an *aha* falls flat. On the other hand, a localization-driven content strategy is capable of producing meaningful content experiences for its audience(s), creating *aha* moments in Anchorage, Andorra, and Anhui.

Andrew Lawless
Localization Strategy

What is it?

The art and science of planning and directing operations in a global marketplace so that a product or service cannot be distinguished from a local offering. Marshals resources for internationalization, localization, translation, and transcreation for their most efficient and productive use.

Why is it important?

Localization strategy is part of a company's global content strategy and defines how they adapt their products or services for one or more international markets and what financial, vendor, and technology resources they need to do so.

About Andrew Lawless

Andrew Lawless is a best-selling author, performance coach, educator, and consultant. He is laser-focused on inspiring professionals for success. Andrew brings a unique blend of experience in behavioral sciences, publishing, localization, and education. He served as consultant to the FBI's Behavioral Science Unit. In 2015, he presented to the US White House during the Obama administration, and in 2012 testified before the US Senate on the importance of professional development in localization. He is an adjunct professor at the University of Maryland.

Email	andrew@lawless.guide
Website	lawless.guide
Twitter	@rockant_inc
LinkedIn	linkedin.com/in/lawlessandrew/
Facebook	facebook.com/lawlessing/

Why does a business professional need to know this?

Localization strategy involves:

- Defining business goals in international markets, such as revenue, profit, market share, expansion, consolidation, conversions, etc.
- Identifying current obstacles that prevent the organization from efficiently and effectively adapting its products to local needs.
- Developing a plan that includes people, processes, technology, and funds to implement that strategy.
- Implementing the plan, measuring progress, and adjusting the plan accordingly.

A localization strategy requires extensive knowledge about the target market and competitors' positions in that market. Understanding local consumer preferences, cultural, political, and legal frameworks, as well as technical requirements, is also central to satisfying customer needs and wants.

A localization strategy connects localized content with business outcomes[77]. Web analytics have made it easier to assemble a remarkable level of detail, but they aren't the whole story. For example, web reports rarely tie into sales data.

Teams need to make cognitive connections between multiple sets of data so that they can understand the larger strategic picture[76].

Madison Van Doren
Monolingual

What is it?
The ability to speak only one language, including non-verbal languages such as sign languages.

Why is it important?
Language acts as a filter between an individual and the world around them. A monolingual person has only one filter and, therefore, only one perspective for interpreting the world. This has implications for marketing and user experience.

About Madison Van Doren
Madison Van Doren is a recent graduate of Colorado State University with a Bachelor's degree in English with a concentration in Language and a minor in Linguistics. She is pursuing an MA in Linguistics at Queen Mary University of London with research interests in historical and sociolinguistics.

Email   madisonvandoren@gmail.com
LinkedIn   linkedin.com/in/madisonvandoren

Why does a business professional need to know this?

Localization is rooted in accommodating the essential role language plays in everyday life. To meet the linguistic and cultural needs of a population, people involved in localization must understand that the perspective of a monolingual individual or community is different from that of a multilingual individual or community. This different perspective can affect how marketing messages are interpreted, as well as the overall user experience.

A monolingual community often differs in how in-group and out-group status is established. These communities might define their in-group based on assimilation with the dominant language of the monolingual population, or divide communities by language if multiple monolingual groups exist.

A current example of this can be seen in the UK, where monolingual refugees struggle to find their place in dominant English-speaking communities. If the language of a monolingual community or individual is not that of the dominant society, then the immigrant community could be ostracized or pressured to assimilate. In this situation, these communities might require different marketing messages or information than the dominant culture that surrounds them[85].

The perspectives of monolingual speakers are varied, but can be accommodated by localization specialists if handled carefully[87].

Berry Braster
Multilingual

What is it?

The use of more than one language in communication.

Why is it important?

Without multilingualism, there would no localization. In a world where products and services are sold globally, companies must translate and adapt their messages in a way that is locally understood if they want to succeed in the global market.

About Berry Braster

Berry Braster has been in the industry of technical documentation and translations since 2001 and has consulted and implemented various types of content strategies, including Simplified Technical English and the HyperSTE content checker software, with many companies representing many types of industries. He is currently the Technology Director of Technical Documentation at Etteplan, overseeing R&D and various types of technologies, including content management, spare parts catalogs, dynamic viewers, and augmented reality.

Email	berry.braster@etteplan.com
Website	technicaldocumentation.services
Twitter	@berrybraster
LinkedIn	linkedin.com/in/berrybraster/

Why does a business professional need to know this?

Multilingual speakers significantly outnumber monolingual speakers in the world's population[90]. As an example, more than half of Europeans speak more than one language, and although English is considered as the most commonly used language in international communication, it ranks lower than Spanish and Chinese as the most spoken language[88].

Therefore, companies must always consider using more than one language when communicating with an international audience. Companies must also ensure that they communicate in a way that is understandable for everyone, regardless of technical, cultural, or language background. Lack of clarity can cause misunderstandings, with sometimes dangerous consequences. And mistakes are easily made, considering that some words can have hundreds of different definitions.

For technical documentation, many countries and regions require content to be translated into the local language, which means that companies must ensure that the original meaning translates correctly while weighing the cost of that translation and the potential value of a particular market.

Standardizing the source language can facilitate translation and help to ensure consistency. Specifications, such as Simplified Technical English (STE)[91], can help remove ambiguity from the source content, making it easier to translate. However, this brings up another challenge because not all authors are native English speakers, and some might be less familiar with some of the nuances of meaning. These authors need a good command of English to write in STE, but with training they can be successful.

Alan J. Porter
Native Speaker

What is it?

Someone who has naturally used a language from an early age as a primary means of concept formation and communication rather than acquiring the language later in life.

Why is it important?

Being a native speaker implies a high level of *fluency* in a specific language, and native speakers are often chosen to translate texts into that language based on this assumption.

About Alan J. Porter

Driven to educate, inform, and entertain through content, Alan J. Porter is an industry leading content strategist. He is author of *The Content Pool* [14] and a regular conference speaker, workshop leader, and writer on content marketing, content strategy, customer experience, brand management, and content and localization strategy.

Email	ajp@4jsgroup.com
Website	thecontentpool.com
Twitter	@thecontentpool
LinkedIn	linkedin.com/in/alanjporter
Facebook	facebook.com/TheContentPool

Why does a business professional need to know this?

Speaking like a native of any language means more than just knowing vocabulary and grammar. Signs of a native speaker include instantly understanding what slang means, what cultural references mean, and how to reduce syntax to a bare minimum, while still conveying precise meaning. Native speakers do not, however, always speak according to the rules of their standard national languages. They display regional, occupational, generational, and social class-related ways of talking.

Most native speakers have a vocabulary of at least 30,000 to 40,000 words in their internalized language and are often assumed to have a certain level of fluency, given the ability to recognize context as well as meaning[95]. Therefore, such native speakers frequently are used to translate into their native language. However, one can argue that they might not be the best person to translate that text, as not all native speakers are proficient in their native languages. Often, those who have received an education in a second language are more likely to be proficient in its formal grammar and structures.

The increase in multilingual speakers and the spread of languages across borders, combined with digital globalization, has blurred the definition of what exactly it means to be a native speaker[96] [97] [98].

Hans Fenstermacher
Source Language

What is it?
The original language that content is created in and from which translation takes place.

Why is it important?
The source language carries the original meaning and intent of a communication, as created by the content author, that is then conveyed in the process of translation.

About Hans Fenstermacher
Hans Fenstermacher is a 35-year veteran of the language industry, beginning his career as a translator and interpreter in 7 languages. In 2002, he co-founded GALA (Globalization and Localization Association), the world's largest trade association for language companies. After selling his language business to TransPerfect in 2006, Hans served as global Vice President there until 2012, when he became CEO of GALA for a 2-year stint. Today, Hans is an executive at United Language Group.

Email   hansfenstermacher@gmail.com
Twitter   @Hansfens
LinkedIn   linkedin.com/in/hansfenstermacher

Why does a business professional need to know this?

The source language contains the meaning, intent, and substance of the communication of original content (e.g., a text message, software app, website, documentation, audio, video, etc.) that will be conveyed into one or more *target languages*. Together, the source and target form a *language pair*, which is the basis for all translation.

Before rendering the meaning of source content into a target language, translators must be *fluent* in the source language, and *native speakers* of the target language. Translators must understand the text perfectly, including specialized terminology, tone, speech register, style, and more. In addition to this linguistic precision, translators must also grasp the purpose of the message and the desired outcome for the recipient, as well as understand the context of the content and how it can affect meaning. A marketing piece is worded differently than instructions in a machine operator's manual, and a different outcome is expected. For a marketing piece, the content author might tolerate ambiguity because the aim is affinity and a call to action. For an operator's manual, precision and clarity are most important.

In addition to meaning, the source language determines a critical aspect of localization: cost. Typically, translation is priced by the source word (this is because the volume of target words can vary widely, depending on the target language and the translation itself)[118]. This makes it especially important to control the volume and consistency of source language words as much as possible[116] [117].

Fabiano Cid
Target language

What is it?

The language into which a product is localized.

Why is it important?

You cannot talk about translation, which is at the core of the localization process, without defining the target language(s) because this will guide the decision of which audience you intend to reach.

About Fabiano Cid

Fabiano Cid is the Managing Director of Ccaps Translation and Localization, a company that supports the language needs of global brands in Latin America. He has 20 years of localization experience and is an active member of the language industry. He is currently involved in the Gender Equality Project. Fabiano is the co-creator of Think Latin America, a former Globalization and Localization Association (GALA) Ambassador, Board Member, and Chair. He has also served as the chairman of the Milengo corporate board.

Email	fcid@ccaps.net
Website	ccaps.net
Twitter	@fabcid
LinkedIn	linkedin.com/in/fabianocid
Facebook	facebook.com/FabianoCcaps

Why does a business professional need to know this?

A single *source language* can be rendered into one or more target languages, depending on the budget and scope of reach. The process of translation and localization creates the content in the target language by rendering software code, website, game, audio, video, or any other localizable content so that end users can read, listen, and make the most of their experience. The combination of a source language plus a target language and its locale creates a *language pair*.

Before planning a *localization strategy*, you must define your target audience and the language(s) they speak. Typically, companies select the target languages and locales based on the markets that they want to reach with a particular product.

Make sure that the translators are well-versed in the target language (preferably native speakers), because they must have the capacity to render the meaning of the original text into the translated text, making sure that the translated test meets the following criteria:

- Reads as fluent.
- Follows the linguistic characteristics of the locale.
- Incorporates terminology preferences of the target audience.
- Obeys stylistic choices.
- Uses industry jargon correctly.
- Meets local requirements, including those of a legal or regulatory nature.

Lori Thicke
Translation (t9n)

What is it?
The act of rendering content from one language into another, accurately reproducing not just the meaning but the tone as well.

Why is it important?
Translation makes content accessible to people who speak a different language, increasing both understanding and impact.

About Lori Thicke
Lori Thicke founded the language services provider Lexcelera as well as its subsidiary, the machine translation innovator LexWorks. Today, Lexcelera has offices in Paris, London, Vancouver, Singapore, and Buenos Aires. Lori also founded the world's largest humanitarian translation organization, Translators without Borders. Lori, who holds an MFA from the University of British Columbia, lives in Paris, and is a frequent speaker and blogger on bridging the language divide.

Email	lori@lexcelera.com
Website	lexcelera.com
Twitter	@lorithicke
LinkedIn	linkedin.com/in/lorithicke
Facebook	facebook.com/lori.thicke

Why does a business professional need to know this?

Translation is the window that opens up content to a wider audience. But it's about more than simply increasing understanding. Translating content into the right language allows users to connect more deeply with it. As Nelson Mandela famously said, "If you talk to a man in a language he understands, that goes to his head. If you talk to him in his language, that goes to his heart."

This deeper connection with your content can increase engagement and loyalty, as well as sales and even profitability. The independent research firm, Common Sense Advisory (CSA), has identified a strong correlation between a brand's financial strength and the number of languages on its website[140]. Other studies have found that customers addressed in their own language are much more likely to make online purchases[141]. The CSA also equates language with a positive customer experience[142].

Multilingual content improves user experience, drives sales, and creates loyalty. It also boosts profits by leveraging the investments that have already been made in research, design, production, marketing, and branding. Translation, once seen as solely as a cost center, is actually an investment in the local market and the customer.

 **Advanced**

Arle Lommel
Augmented Translation

What is it?

A form of human translation carried out within an integrated technology environment that provides translators access to sub-segment, adaptive *machine translation (MT)* and *translation memory (TM)*, terminology lookup, and automatic content enrichment (ACE) to aid their work, and that automates project management, file handling, and other ancillary tasks.

Why is it important?

Augmented translation makes translators more efficient by automatically handling routine and repetitive tasks, and freeing them to focus on difficult content that requires human attention.

About Arle Lommel

Arle Lommel is a senior analyst with Common Sense Advisory (CSA Research), where he focuses on language technology and translation quality. A noted writer and speaker on localization and translation, he headed standards development at the Localization Industry Standards Association (LISA) and later at GALA, before working on translation quality topics at the German Research Center for Artificial Intelligence (DFKI). He has a PhD from Indiana University and currently resides in Bloomington, Indiana.

Email	arle.lommel@gmail.com
Website	commonsenseadvisory.com
Twitter	@ArleLommel
LinkedIn	linkedin.com/in/arlelommel/

Why does a business professional need to know this?

Augmented translation gives translators access to various technologies in a unified environment. The central component is adaptive machine translation that learns from translators in real time. It extends translators' capabilities by reusing their own work more efficiently and lets them focus on new and difficult content.

In addition, augmented translation combines the following:

- terminology identification and disambiguation that links to authoritative references with information and translations.
- automated content enrichment (ACE) that provides links to related resources, such as court decisions in a legal translation.
- translation memory that supports both machine translation and traditional methodologies.
- project management that automatically coordinates activities and shares information between all parties.

As of 2017, no environment incorporates all of these elements, but the individual components are becoming increasingly common, and some platforms already include some of them. As augmented translation technology evolves, it will make translators more efficient, productive, and valuable[1] [2].

Diana Ballard
Localization Project Management System (LPMS)

What is it?

A collaborative platform to increase localization efficiency by managing, automating, and reporting the workflow, as well as by centrally storing, organizing, and processing language resources and assets.

Why is it important?

A localization project management system (LPMS) is essential for accelerating and scaling localization productivity and consistency, and bringing stakeholders together. When implemented properly, It unifies and automates processes, governance, and strategy, as well as centralizing language resources.

About Diana Ballard

With over 30 years in international business, Diana Ballard has wide experience in manufacturing and service industries, delivering business consultancy, setting up new projects, and expanding markets. She specializes in supporting customers in global readiness and in executing successful localization and translation initiatives. Diana currently leads business development at STAR USA (STAR Group), the leading information management, language services company with a high performance suite of technologies to unify the end-to-end information lifecycle.

Email	diana.ballard@star-group.net
Website	star-usa.com
Twitter	@DianaBallard18
LinkedIn	linkedin.com/in/diana-ballard-b430509
Facebook	facebook.com/diana.ballard.35

Why does a business professional need to know this?

An LPMS allows companies to manage growing localization demands, volume, and complexity. Implementing an LPMS not only improves efficiency and automation, it allows companies to gain more control over their process and their *translation memories (TM)*, as well as scale their localization spend based on market demand.

These systems have evolved from client-server or web server systems to cloud services, and they scale to support the full range of language service providers. Workbenches provide role-based dashboards with automated messaging and workflow management.

System capabilities, customization, and configuration vary, but typically include these features:

- **Business Management:**
  - project management
  - vendor or client management
  - financial control and accounting
- **Process Management:**
  - workflow configurations for diverse business needs
  - change management
  - support for different methodologies (waterfall, *Agile*, etc.)
  - content processing that facilitates organization, management, allocation, and automation of the supply chain
- **File/Content Exchange:** options range from manual file transfer (file upload, SFTP) to automated exchange via system connectors using web services and programmatic interfaces.
- **Language Processing and Analysis:**
  - support for multiple content types and formats
  - centralized language assets
  - company or third-party linguistic review
  - integrated *machine translation*
- **Analytics and Reporting:**
  - service performance (time, quality, metrics) with trends
  - costs, including re-use analysis
  - status reporting of schedules and tasks
  - governance and quality management

LPMSes can have wider application to foster knowledge sharing across languages or to apply *Computer Assisted Translation (CAT)* tools in authoring environments, which promotes reuse in the original language. This, in turn, increases reuse in translation and lowers translation costs.

Don DePalma
Machine Translation (MT)

What is it?
A software-based process that translates content from one language to another without human intervention. People may be involved in training software for specific domains or *post-editing* the output for linguistic quality or style.

Why is it important?
Machine translation accelerates the process, and reduces the cost, of translating content and increases the availability of translated content. Linguistic quality and accuracy levels vary, depending on how well the software is tuned and whether the content is *post-edited* by humans.

About Don DePalma
Don DePalma is an industry analyst, author, and corporate strategist with expertise in business- and marketing-focused technology. Don regularly publishes syndicated research, authors articles, and contributes to a blog at http://commonsenseadvisory.com/Blogs.aspx.

He lectures and writes on the topics of global business, cross-border marketing, application and content management, global customer experience, and globalization.

Email	don@csa-research.com
Website	commonsenseadvisory.com
Twitter	@CSA_Research
LinkedIn	linkedin.com/in/dondepalma/

Why does a business professional need to know this?

Business professionals should care about machine translation (MT) based on the numbers. Far too much content is being created and far too few translators or money exist to translate it all – or even a small fraction of it – into the dozens of languages that are required to address major global markets.

Translation automation tools, such as MT, promise to increase the volume and accelerate the pace of words rendered into other languages. Understanding this dynamic puts business professionals in a better position to take advantage of what's happening with this core technology.

Translation strategies that rely on human output alone have already been overwhelmed by the explosion in content and the imperative to rapidly enter new markets. If business professionals are going to meet the needs of their many users, they will have to evaluate how to integrate MT into their global content strategies, regardless of the type or size of their organization[82] [83].

Richard Brooks
Multilingual Search Engine Optimization (MSEO)

What is it?
The art of optimizing a website so search results for the site appear in search engines, regardless of language or region. Also known as international search engine optimization (ISEO).

Why is it important?
Allows content to be found and consumed by more people than the nearest competitor by increasing findability in search engines result pages, regardless of the language of search.

About Richard Brooks
Richard Brooks is the CEO of K International. He holds an MBA from Cranfield School of Management and is a former board member for the Association of Language Companies. He is an experienced professional in the localization industry, much respected for his business insight and acumen. He is a popular international conference and event speaker, building a reputation by using an open, passionate, and honest style to keep audiences engaged.

Email	Richard.Brooks@k-international.com
Website	k-international.com
Twitter	@RichardMBrooks
LinkedIn	linkedin.com/in/richardbrooks/

Why does a business professional need to know this?

The investment in great online content offers a superior return on investment (ROI) only if that content is available to consumers, regardless of language or location. However, simply translating your content isn't enough. People can't engage with your content if they can't find it. As Willy Brandt said, "If I'm selling to you, I speak your language. If I'm buying from you, dann müssen Sie Deutsch sprechen."

Copy, localized or otherwise, starts with keywords. Using the right metadata, you can gain insights into what is being searched, where it's being searched, the frequency of searches, and the level of competition. The Google Keyword Tool[92] provides a wealth of information for free. Armed with this information, you can ensure that your content has a greater chance of being relevant and useful in the regions you're targeting.

Also consider where you host your content. Hosting on a local domain – for example, *domain.de* if you are selling in Germany – can improve trust. However, this increases your workload, so be careful to select a web content management system that can handle local domains easily.

Once the content is in place, the process of reaching out to local bloggers and social media magnates in their own language can begin. Manually adding your site to local, respected business directories will gain trust, as will carefully constructing local social media pages for your company.

Over time, localized pages will appear in the search engines. Using your measurements and feedback loops, you can determine the strategies that work best in each region to gain prominent placement in search engine results across multiple languages[93].

Todd Resnick
Multilingual Voice Over

What is it?

The scripted audio recording of human voices speaking in multiple languages; the spoken word applied to media.

Why is it important?

Multilingual voice over provides a way to communicate globally and in a unified way through various media. Many business applications use recorded voice. Narration is a common style of voice over that is frequently used for multilingual voice over recordings. Narration is known for its slower tempo, which allows you to hear the texture of a relaxed vocal reading clearly.

About Todd Resnick

Todd Resnick is a world-renowned voice over director who has overseen the production of many storied franchises in entertainment, e-learning, and industrial use of video products. He has personally managed and hired talent across 90+ languages for voice over, subtitling, desktop publishing, and platform engineering.

Email	todd.resnick@thevoiceco.com
Website	resnickinteractive.com
Twitter	@toddresnick
LinkedIn	linkedin.com/in/toddresnick/
Facebook	facebook.com/ResnickTodd

Why does a business professional need to know this?

As more and more global brands explore the need to create multimedia content, understanding the issues and considerations surrounding management of the human voice – especially across cultures and languages – is going to become a critical differentiator. Brands that do it well will be able to provide relevant customer experiences to prospects and customers alike.

Because of this trend, companies need to build voice over into their global content strategy. Precise spoken-word brand messaging is critical to effective market penetration, regulatory compliance, human resources training, elearning, sales, technical support, phone menus, and more.

Voice is the most intimate and memorable format of knowledge transfer. When voice is done with precision and professional quality, people absorb it and are drawn to it. When done poorly, people repel from it.

Entertainment and business video multilingual voice over is about acting (playing a specific role) and *transcreation* (on the fly adaptation to ensure the voice over matches the intent and the character for which voice over is being provided). The actors are not just translating, they are playing the role of the character they are providing an alternative voice for. It's about authenticity and believability, and, much like localization, it involves more than just the words.

For multilingual voice over, transcreation requires that you develop a character and enforce consistency and fidelity across every touchpoint in every language. In addition, you have to consider how cultural differences and expectations might affect the way the character is portrayed[94].

Tony O'Dowd
Natural Language Processing (NLP)

What is it?

The branch of artificial intelligence (AI) and computational linguistics that deals with the analysis, representation, processing, and synthesis of written and spoken human languages.

Why is it important?

NLP has important implications in the ways that humans and computers work together and how we bridge the gap between human language and digital data. While many applications already use NLP, as we progress with artificial intelligence, it will become even more important.

About Tony O'Dowd

Tony O'Dowd is currently the Founder and Chief Architect of Kantan-MT.com, which is a market leader in enterprise level machine translation solutions. He has over 30 years' experience working in the localization industry and has held positions at Lotus Development Corporation, Symantec Corporation, Corel Corporation Ltd., and Alchemy Software Development, which he founded in 2000.

Email	tonyod@kantanmt.com
Website	kantanmt.com/
Twitter	@KantanMT
LinkedIn	ie.linkedin.com/in/tonyo3
Facebook	facebook.com/KantanMT/

Why does a business professional need to know this?

NLP plays a central role in a wide range of applications today. For example, many spam filters use a technique called *Bayesian filtering*. This is a statistical approach in which the frequency of certain words are measured against the distribution of similar words in a collection of known spam email messages. Using this approach, we can calculate the probability that a message is spam based on its content. We can use a similar approach to detect the language of a tweet or a website by measuring character distributions.

Another NLP technique, central to every web search, attempts to extract meaning from texts. For example, using NLP techniques, we can recognize search queries, extract the meaning, and provide answers that are contextually relevant to the user. Further refinement of these techniques allow us to summarize the meaning of documents and to develop sentiment analysis, a method of identifying and categorizing opinions in a piece of text to determine whether the attitude of the writer is positive, negative, or neutral. This analysis determines how the launch of a new product is perceived by the market.

Machine translation (MT) is another important application of NLP. The biggest challenge in MT is not translating words, but preserving the meaning of the sentence. This is a complex technological challenge that is at the heart of NLP research today. *Neural MT* is better at preserving the meaning of a sentence and, consequently, generates better and more fluent translations.

NLP is at the heart of how we currently interact with computer systems and will drive the next evolution in how we interact with them in the future.

Localization
Engineering

Lydia Clarke
Alignment (of a TM)

What is it?

A two-step process used to ensure that previous translations are correctly matched to the original source in the *translation memory (TM)*. First, the software matches existing translations with their original source. Second, a linguist confirms the matching of source to target.

Why is it important?

Alignment is a great way to retain previous translations that were not completed using a translation memory tool. Done correctly, alignment preserves previous language work and ports it into a reusable format.

About Lydia Clarke

Lydia Clarke leads Acclaro's San Francisco team to deliver unmatched localization and translation services. Lydia's long experience across the localization industry helps her to guide clients through strategic decisions to reach their long-term globalization goals.

Lydia holds a BA from Cornell University in Spanish and International Relations. When not at work, Lydia spends time with her family (1 husband, 3 kids, 2 dogs). Rare moments of solitude are reserved for cooking, reading, hiking, and singing.

Email	lclarke@acclaro.com
Website	acclaro.com
Twitter	@LydiaJClarke
LinkedIn	linkedin.com/in/lydia-clarke-localization

Why does a business professional need to know this?

Suppose you are embarking on a translation effort with a team of professional linguists who will use a unified translation memory system. You have some translations already; that content is live, and your internal team is happy with it, but it wasn't done using a translation memory (TM) tool. Can you salvage that work? The answer is yes, with alignment.

Alignment is a two-step process matching previous translations to original source, *segment* by segment. The texts are aligned by a TM tool first, and then by a linguist who confirms or corrects the matches the tool has proposed. This verification ensures that the source and target are correctly aligned and allows those previous translations to be reused as leverage for future translation work.

It's important to note that alignment is not an exact science, and if the source and target don't match exactly, not all content will align into the TM. Also, if there is any question of the quality of the translations, it's smart to edit the translated content before you populate your translation memory with it.

Linguistic alignment can be expensive, depending on how much content you have and how closely the source and target content line up. It's worth evaluating the *Return on Investment (ROI)* before embarking on any major effort. But if you're happy with previous translation work that was done outside of TM, it can be worthwhile to align that content into a TM so you can continue to put it to use.

Chase Tingley
Character Encoding

What is it?

A method for representing characters in a data format, typically binary, so that the characters can be transmitted electronically and decoded properly by the receiver.

Why is it important?

As localizers, all the text we work with is encoded for storage and transmission. If we don't know how it's encoded, we'll read or write it incorrectly.

About Chase Tingley

Chase Tingley is VP of Engineering at Spartan Software, Inc. He has 15 years of experience developing localization tools, including work on WorldServer, GlobalSight, and Ontram. An advocate for the greater adoption of localization standards and open source tools, he is a core contributor to the Okapi Framework (open source framework for creating interoperable localization tools, http://okapi.sourceforge.net/) and a member of the OASIS XLIFF and XLIFF-OMOS Technical Committees.

Email	chase@spartansoftwareinc.com
Website	spartansoftwareinc.com/
Twitter	@ctatwork
LinkedIn	linkedin.com/in/ctingley/

Why does a business professional need to know this?

If two people exchange handwritten letters, they can be reasonably confident that if one writes the letter "A," the other will recognize it. But what if they send those messages electronically? The sender and receiver have to agree in advance how the sender should convert the text to binary data, so the receiver can reverse the process and read what was sent.

That agreement is a character encoding: a system to map characters to a transmission format, and back. Character encoding predates computers (Morse code is one example), but in localization, we are primarily concerned with encoding characters to binary.

If text is stored using one encoding method and read back using a different method, corrupted characters will result. To reduce this risk, many applications always use the same encoding, but it's still perilously easy for buggy localization tools to accidentally corrupt data during processing.

Historically, the term *character encoding* has been used interchangeably with *character set*, but with the rise of *Unicode*, it's important to maintain the distinction, because Unicode is a single character set that supports multiple character encodings. That is, Unicode data can be stored in different ways (*UTF-8*, UTF-16, etc.), and you need to know which method was used. In general, knowing the character encoding is enough to infer the character set, but the converse is not always true.

If you're lucky, you should rarely need to interact with character encodings directly[5] [6].

Dave Ruane
Character Set

What is it?

A defined list of grouped symbols used for digital communication.

Why is it important?

All global text belongs to a particular character set. Digital programs and platforms expect a specific character set so that they correctly process, render, and visualize each character of the text.

About Dave Ruane

Dave Ruane is part of the enterprise business team at Xplanation Language Services. His current interests are Agile methodologies, global continuous delivery methods, and creating customer experience through global content. His background is in localization engineering, and he has been in the industry since the mid-1990s. He is a frequent speaker at industry events and is the creator of the Process Innovation Challenge, a platform for developing and showcasing innovation in the industry.

Email	dave.ruane@xplanation.com
Website	xplanation.com
Twitter	@DaveRuaneSpain
LinkedIn	linkedin.com/in/davidruane/

Why does a business professional need to know this?

In its simplest form, a character set is a mapping (table) between text characters and the binary numbers that a computer or other digital device understands. For example, the 3 letters "A, B, C" are read as "01000001, 01000010, 01000011" by a computer using the ASCII character set (one of the early character sets).

As the need for global software arose in the 1980s and 1990s, computer scientists devised digital character sets that could manage character complexity and the thousands of characters in languages such as Chinese. Some character sets assigned a single byte to characters and others used double or multiple bytes for each character. Vendor- and platform-specific character sets also became common and created situations where similar character sets had different values for the same character, which meant that characters would be rendered incorrectly if processed using the mapping for the wrong character set[7].

If an application supports a specific character set, the user's device needs to recognize and support the same character set, as part of the due diligence for publishing globally.

For this reason, software localization and development engineers must understand character sets[8]. Issues with character sets can be the bane of their lives, especially when character corruption occurs – for example, when translated software strings are moved across platforms that support different character sets or *character encodings* (e.g. from UNIX to Windows).

Today, more harmonization exists in this area with the proliferation of *Unicode* [9] (which assigns a unique number to every character in nearly every language) and its various character encodings. A character set can have multiple character encodings, but each encoding can relate to only one character set[10].

Jost Zetzsche
Computer-aided translation (CAT)

What is it?

A translation process in which professional human translators use software programs, such as *translation memory* or *terminology management* tools, that support and facilitate productivity and accurate, consistent translations.

Why is it important?

CAT tools provide workflow management and resource allocation and help human translators build and maintain translation memories. When implemented correctly, CAT tools significantly improve efficiency, quality, and consistency, which helps to reduce translation costs.

About Jost Zetzsche

Jost Zetzsche is a translation technology consultant, an author on various aspects of translation, and an ATA-certified English-to-German technical translator. He earned a PhD in the field of Chinese translation history and linguistics at the University of Hamburg. His computer guide for translators is now in its thirteenth edition[12], and his technical journal for the translation industry goes out to more than 11,000 translation professionals. He is co-author, with Nataly Kelly, of *Found in Translation: How Translation Shapes Our Lives and Transforms the World* [65].

Email	jzetzsche@internationalwriters.com
Website	internationalwriters.com/
Twitter	@jeromobot
LinkedIn	linkedin.com/in/jostzetzsche/

Why does a business professional need to know this?

With computer-aided translation (CAT), translators use computer software to support the translation process. Such tools are core components in a professional translator's toolbox and are key to a translator's ability to deliver consistent quality on time and on budget.

Translators typically use multi-featured software suites or CAT tools (also referred to as translation environment tools or, less accurately, TM tools), but there are also many smaller applications that specialize in just one of the necessary features.

Most full-fledged CAT tools offer these features:

- access and management of translation memories (including *alignment*, i.e., the conversion of already translated texts into translation memories)
- terminology databases
- *machine translation*
- quality assurance
- file and project management
- separation of translatable text from untranslatable code in all common file formats.

Most CAT tools also support data exchange of translation memories, termbases, and translation files through XML-based exchange standards such as *TMX*, *TBX*, and *XLIFF*.

Today, most CAT tools are either hybrid solutions, where some components can be shared through web-based access, or completely web-based. While they are still predominantly built for professional translators, some tools – for example, Google Translator Toolkit[92], Wikipedia's Content Translation tool, or tools that support crowd-sourced translation – are also used by non-professional translators and volunteers[11] [12].

Chris Norton
Desktop Publishing (DTP)

What is it?

The production of professional quality, print-ready materials using specialized software to design the layouts and templates. It has replaced manual typesetting and paste up as a discipline, and has evolved beyond desktop computers to include laptops, mobile devices, and the cloud.

Why is it important?

DTP software is used to produce most printed documentation in circulation. It can be 50% of the cost of a localization project, so if the source files are poorly internationalized, this task can break a company's localization budget[128]. Properly implemented XML or other structure can significantly reduce DTP costs, but you still need skilled designers to create the output templates.

About Chris Norton

Chris Norton has an Honours degree in Typography and Graphic Communication from Reading University where he also developed early SGML processes. Since graduating in the late 1980s, Chris has worked mostly in the localization industry, helping to develop early versions of most of the processes in standard use today. He has worked on most types of documentation imaginable and, in doing so, has used all the different DTP software available in a professional capacity.

Email   chris.norton@ukdtp.com

Why does a business professional need to know this?

The proliferation and evolution of DTP applications presents a business challenge to localization vendors and clients alike with regard to evaluating, purchasing, maintaining, and managing training for these tools.

As DTP applications evolved, the industry developed processes to efficiently extract formatted text from DTP tools for processing by *computer-aided translation (CAT)* systems.

Content developers use DTP software to create the source. The localization team extracts the textual elements, passes them through the translation process, then re-integrates the text back into the original DTP software for final production of the *target language* versions.

In a perfect world, this round trip would require no modifications to the layout post-translation, but this is rarely the case. Poorly designed templates, layouts, and graphic designs often lead to a lot of re-work after the translated content has been re-integrated.

While many DTP applications also support output to online deliverables, DTP as a discipline (particularly in localization) focuses on print-ready content and requires knowledge of design and typography best practices.

In localization, DTP works best when the content is intelligently created and well-internationalized, beginning with using a DTP localization expert to create source templates. Without such expertise, and even with the most capable software, you are likely to end up with badly designed and poorly created documentation that will cost significant time and money to localize.

Many documentation developers are switching to content management systems rather than traditional DTP software, but DTP software still remains an integral part of the documentation production process for most printed material.

Val Swisher
Exact match

What is it?

The instance when a source *segment* that is submitted to translation is word-for-word the same as a source segment that has already been translated and exists in the *translation memory (TM)*.

Why is it important?

Exact matches save translation expenses. Once a segment has been translated, an exact match reduces the cost of processing that same segment again. In-context exact matches reduce costs even more.

About Val Swisher

Val Swisher is the CEO of Content Rules. Val helps companies solve complex content problems by analyzing their content and how it is created. She is a well-known expert in structured authoring, global content strategy, content development, and terminology management. Val thinks that content should be easy to read, cost-effective to translate, and efficient to manage. Her third book, *Global Content Strategy: A Primer* [115], was published in 2014 by XML Press.

Email	vals@contentrules.com
Website	contentrules.com
Twitter	@valswisher
LinkedIn	linkedin.com/in/valswisher

Why does a business professional need to know this?

Exact match is a concept that is closely tied to *translation memory*. Translation memory (TM) is a database that stores completed translations so they can be reused for future projects. When a segment is translated, the source segment and the translated equivalent are stored together as a translation unit in the TM[27].

When a translator receives additional content to translate, new segments are compared to the existing translation units. If a new source segment and its translation already exist in the TM, the cost for translating the new segment is minimized. The closer the match between the new and previous source segments, the lower the cost. If the source segments match exactly, the cost is minimal[28].

If the segment before and after any given segment are also exact matches, there may be no charge to translate the new segment at all. This is called an in-context exact match[29] [30].

As a by-product of updating existing content, words are sometimes changed from one version to the next for purely stylistic reasons. The changes add no informational value and can cause what could be an exact match to become *fuzzy* and, therefore, more expensive to translate. This is a waste of money. In addition to saving money, exact matches have other positive effects on both the source and target languages:

- Content that is consistent is easier to read.
- Content that is consistent is easier to re-use.
- Content that is consistent is easier to update.

Julie Walker
Fuzzy Match

What is it?

The instance when a source segment that is submitted to translation is partially recognized as being similar to a source segment that has already been translated and exists in the *translation memory (TM)*.

Why is it important?

Fuzzy match is important for translation costs and efficiency. As a TM builds up a library of content, it will recognize more fuzzy matches, leading to reduced costs and increased efficiency.

About Julie Walker

Julie Walker is a freelance marketing and technical writer. She helps businesses tell their story by writing engaging and educational content that customers can find online. Previously, Julie was a technical communication manager for a global company for 13 years, managing the localization process, content lifecycles, and technical writers. She implemented an XML, task-based authoring, publishing, and translation system that significantly reduced their translation costs.

Email	julie@wordstellastory.com
Website	wordstellastory.com
LinkedIn	linkedin.com/in/juliewalker1/

Why does a business professional need to know this?

For localization, you want to reuse existing translated content as much as possible to reduce costs, increase consistency, and improve time to market.

A TM helps with content reuse. When you submit source content to a localization service provider (LSP) for an estimate, they will run the content through a TM to leverage the existing translations.

The LSP typically provides three types of quotes:

- *exact match* (least expensive)
- fuzzy match (more expensive than an exact match, less expensive than a new word)
- new word (most expensive)

Here is a fuzzy match example. The segment, "She's an expert skier," exists in the TM. Your new content contains the *segment*, "She's an expert snowboarder." The TM recognizes the segment as an 80% fuzzy match because the words *skier* and *snowboarder* are different in each segment. The translator reviews the context to determine whether to accept or modify the fuzzy match.

As you add content with each project, the TM finds more fuzzy and exact matches and fewer new words, which reduces translation costs. The efficiency of the translation process also increases because the TM pre-populates the content for the translators to review for context. The more previously translated content that can be pre-populated, the less translation time required and the faster the time to market.

You can increase the number of fuzzy and exact matches by defining and using consistent terminology in the *source* and *target* languages, implementing a content reuse strategy, and using a controlled language like Simplified Technical English[91].

Bert Esselink
Localization Engineering

What is it?
Technical activities required to support the process of translation, including converting files to a translatable format, re-converting them to their original formats after translation, and ensuring technical validity of translated files.

Why is it important?
Localization engineering is a key component of the localization process and often included as a cost item in estimates, but it is frequently misunderstood or misinterpreted.

About Bert Esselink
Bert Esselink has been active in multilingual publishing and marketing projects for two decades. He worked for many years as a localization specialist, focusing on project management, language technology, multilingual marketing, and global content management. His book *A Practical Guide to Localization* [128] is used widely throughout the localization and translation industry. After working for many years with Lionbridge in Amsterdam, Bert joined SDL as Strategic Account Director in August 2017.

Email   bert.esselink@gmail.com
LinkedIn   nl.linkedin.com/in/esselin

Why does a business professional need to know this?

Localization engineering affects all stages of a project, from project scoping and preparation to actually building and testing translated deliverables.

During the scoping step, the localization engineer analyzes the source files and generates input for a quote or project schedule. Poorly structured files that lack internationalization can significantly increase localization costs and time. Identifying these issues early in the process makes it easier to generate a more accurate estimate and identify training opportunities.

For most technical localization projects, source files come in a structured format such as XML or a strings file for user interface or app localization. Localization engineers convert these files to prepare them for the most efficient translation process. They also ensure that the structure of the translated deliverables is still valid post-translation.

For projects involving user support and marketing content, the source files can be unstructured word processing, DTP, or HTML files, or they could be in XML, DITA, or another structured format. The localization engineer makes sure that templates and formatting software work in every language for the output format. Some applications provide better localization support than others, so the localization engineer must develop work-arounds for special situations.

With projects that use *Agile development methodologies*, localization engineers are often asked to build scripts or configure automated workflows to process a continuous stream of content and string updates that require rapid turnaround.

Companies can reduce costs by ensuring that the templates and source files are optimized for localization and by providing a *localization kit* to the vendor for each project[75].

Laura Brandon
Post-editing

What is it?

The process whereby a human translator edits machine-translated output to achieve an acceptable level of quality in the final product.

Why is it important?

Machine translation (MT) is frequently used in the translation industry because of its gains in speed and scale. Yet, there is often a loss in quality. Human post-editing improves MT output, bringing the quality up to acceptable levels.

About Laura Brandon

Laura Brandon is the Executive Director of the Globalization and Localization Association (GALA). She oversees operations, staffing, and programming for the association of over 400 member companies in 50+ countries. Laura currently serves on the advisory board of the Localization Certification Program for the University of Washington. She has a degree in French from the Agnes Scott College and a "License" in Art History from the Université de Provence.

Email	lbrandon@gala-global.org
Website	gala-global.org
Twitter	@laura_brandon
LinkedIn	linkedin.com/in/laurabrandon/

Why does a business professional need to know this?

Post-editing helps to ensure that content translated using MT makes sense in context and is of appropriate quality. Lack of post-editing can result in poor customer experience and even legal issues. If your localization strategy includes MT, it also needs to include guidelines for determining which content requires post-editing and under what circumstances.

Machine translation is used throughout the translation and localization sector on a variety of *language pairs* and content types. It is especially useful when you need to translate vast amounts of information quickly. The gains in speed and scale, however, are often offset by losses in fidelity and quality.

Practitioners use many tactics to improve MT output:

- properly training and tuning their MT systems
- ensuring that the source text is well-written and conforms to authoring best practices
- leveraging *terminology management* properly.

Even with these efforts, however, MT output often requires human post-editing to achieve the customer's desired level of quality.

Localization professionals understand that the finished product must be fit for purpose, and this determines the type of post-editing used. For translations that simply need to be good enough (e.g., internal reports), light post-editing is sufficient. For translations of a publishable quality (e.g., customer-facing documentation or web content), full post-editing is required.

Only rarely can raw MT output be used without any post-editing. Both the quality of the raw MT output and the desired quality of the finished product have an impact on time and cost—factors that have an impact on the success of every localization project[99] [100].

Erik Vogt
Script

What is it?

A conventional set of symbols that visually represent sounds and ideas.

Why is it important?

Scripts, or writing systems, are the framework for conveying meaning graphically, and all written words use some form of script. These systems are classified into three types: *logographic*, *syllabic*, and *segmental* [104] [105]. Encoding standards such as ISO/IEC 10646, and *Unicode*, have been developed as a way of representing most, (but certainly not all), scripts in common use today[108]. Of the 7,000+ languages spoken today, roughly a third are considered endangered. Many of these either don't have scripts or are not supported.

About Erik Vogt

Erik Vogt entered the world of translation services as an engineer in 1998 after a variety of jobs, including dabbling in teaching (from ESL to Marine Archaeology), building houses, and installing water lines. Erik has worked with some of the world's most demanding and innovative customers and enjoys bringing it all together, from technology, solving business problems, and supporting team members to be the best at what they do.

Email	erikvo@moravia.com
Website	moravia.com
Twitter	@erikvogt
LinkedIn	linkedin.com/in/erikvogt
Facebook	facebook.com/aerikvogt/

Why does a business professional need to know this?

Scripts are the visual and human-recognizable version of a language. To localize a written language, one must represent the target language in a supported script. Some languages can use more than one script. Serbian, for example, can be written in either Latin or Cyrillic script.

From a technical standpoint, several problems must be solved to display a script. First, the language must be encoded as numbers to be stored and transmitted. This requires *code page* support and at least one input method. There must also be at least one font that can render numbers and the declared code page as recognizable characters. Last, there must be a way to interpret a numerical sequence in a meaningful way.

For example, the order of the characters in a sequence are not always the same as how they need to be displayed, and where a character is displayed in a word or sentence, or the presence of adjacent characters, can modify the shape of a character. In this case, a direct 1:1 mapping of a code point and character is not possible. This can be especially challenging in syllabic and bidirectional scripts.

The Universal Coded Character Set (UCS)[108], with around 136,000 defined characters and a wide range of fonts that support it, has greatly simplified challenges in supporting scripts, but there are still many scripts that remain unsupported, including many rare, obsolete, and fictional languages. For these, and other special cases, creative solutions are still required.

Jamie O'Connell
Segment

What is it?

Phrase, sentence, paragraph, or sentence-like piece of text that represents a cognitive unit and is used when searching for a match in a *translation memory (TM)* database.

Why is it important?

Discrete segments of text show up repeatedly across various pieces of text. Matching source segments in the TM for which previously approved translations exist increases efficiency in the translation process by providing the relevant translation to the translator.

About Jamie O'Connell

Jamie O'Connell is a sales engineer, training manager, and support consultant from Ireland who has been working in the tech sector for over 18 years. He has lived and worked in multiple countries and speaks both English and German. Since 2011, he has been working with 1io, supporting users in their drive for more efficient localization workflows.

Email   jamie.oconnell@gmail.com
Twitter   @mixtwitch
LinkedIn   linkedin.com/in/jamieoc/

Why does a business professional need to know this?

Segments are pieces of text that will be translated as a cognitive unit during a translation workflow; they are typically phrases, sentences, or paragraphs, rather than individual words.

A translation memory (TM) leverages previous translations to avoid duplicating work. Textual content is divided into meaningful segments because it is more likely that a translation will already exist for a smaller segment than for an entire content set. As the TM grows, the number of potentially matching segments increases, reducing translation costs.

To prepare for translation, the software parses new source content into segments based on markup (e.g., XML tags) or a combination of punctuation and white space. Segmentation rules include the punctuation combinations that the software applies during the parsing process.

The translation software then uses the new source segments to search the TM for matches. The translator receives the translated equivalents for editing. For best results, the granularity of the new source segments should be equivalent to the segments in the TM.

The idea of a meaningful segment is important because a segment in one language could have multiple possible translations in another language. Computers are not reliable at discerning meaning in written content. Therefore, the comparison of source segments to segments in the TM typically relies on pattern matching.

However, if three contiguous segments in the source content are 100% matches to three contiguous segments in the TM, the middle segment of the TM is considered an in-context match for meaning and the correct variant, even if other variants exist in the TM[111].

Stefan Gentz
Translation Memory (TM)

What is it?
A repository that contains translated *source* and *target* language pairs.

Why is it important?
Reduces translation time and cost by reusing translated content from the repository. Translation memories are part of a client company's intellectual property.

About Stefan Gentz
As the Worldwide TechComm Evangelist at Adobe, Stefan Gentz's mission is to inspire enterprises and technical writers around the world and show how to create compelling technical communication content with the Adobe Technical Communication Suite of tools. Stefan is a popular speaker at technical communication and translation conferences around the world. He's a certified Quality Management Professional, ISO 9001 / EN 15038 auditor, and Six Sigma Champion. He is also a member of the conference advisory board at tekom / tcworld, the world's largest association for technical communication and ambassador at the Globalization and Localization Association.

Email	gentz@adobe.com
Website	blogs.adobe.com/techcomm/
Twitter	@stefangentz
LinkedIn	linkedin.com/in/stefangentz
Facebook	facebook.com/stefan.gentz

Why does a business professional need to know this?

Professional human translators use *computer-aided translation* tools (CATs) to translate content. A CAT consists of a translation memory, a terminology database, and an editor to translate virtually any kind of content.

During translation, the CAT tool sorts the source language content into small logical units. Such units are usually full sentences (or heading, list item, table cell, etc.) in your content. This unit is called a *segment*. These segments are translated into the target language by a *machine translation* engine, a human translator, or both. Together, a source and target segment form a translation unit (TU), which is stored in a linguistic database called *translation memory (TM)*.

Modern translation memory systems enrich these database entries with additional metadata. Perhaps the most important is metadata that defines the semantic context. Other metadata types include content domain, date and time, translator, quality score, data source, and data type.

When new content is translated, the CAT analyzes each segment and tries to find a match in the TM. Matches can range from no match to *fuzzy* matches to 100%, or *exact*, matches. Modern CAT tools add context matches on top of that: 101% matches that help eliminate false positives due to ambiguities or different context.

With every translation, the TM grows. As the TM grows, more previous translations can be recycled. This dramatically speeds up translation and improves the quality and consistency of new content. Periodically, the TM needs to be reviewed and cleaned to ensure that translation quality stays high.

Terminology Management

Katherine (Kit) Brown-Hoekstra
Controlled Language

What is it?
A curated set of vocabulary selected to communicate clearly and simply for a specific purpose. Controlled language is often used when writing for *machine translation* or for global audiences.

Why is it important?
Controlled language is a critical feature of writing for localization. It is an umbrella term that encompasses several initiatives, including Plain Language, Simplified Technical English, and Caterpillar Fundamental English, among others. Effective controlled language initiatives choose the simplest terms needed to convey meaning, while also restricting grammar, syntax, and verb forms.

About Katherine (Kit) Brown-Hoekstra

Katherine (Kit) Brown-Hoekstra is a Fellow of the Society for Technical Communication (STC), former STC Society President, and a member of the Colorado State University Media Hall of Fame. She is an experienced consultant with over 25 years of experience in technical communication and localization.

As Principal of Comgenesis, LLC, Kit provides consulting and training to her clients on a variety of topics, including localization, content strategy, and content management. She speaks at conferences worldwide and publishes regularly in industry magazines. Her blog is www.pangaeapapers.com.

Email	kit.brown@comgenesis.com
Website	comgenesis.com
Twitter	@kitcomgenesis
LinkedIn	linkedin.com/pub/kit-brown-hoekstra/0/321/71b

Why does a business professional need to know this?

By including controlled language in your global content strategy, you gain significant benefits[16]:

- **Improved comprehensibility:** controlled language can help make content easier to read and understand.
- **Improved consistency and reuse:** when used with structured authoring (e.g., XML) and component-based content management, controlled language can help you maximize reuse.
- **Better terminology management:** controlled language specifications provide an objective starting point for managing terminology, particularly across disciplines[15].
- **Improved quality control and efficiency:** by automating tedious tasks like checking compliance, editors can use their time on higher-value activities, such as improving the internationalization, organization, and intelligence of the content.
- **Improved quantitative metrics:** several tools exist that enable you to track compliance to a controlled language specification. These tools facilitate benchmarking *before* and *after* editing the content for compliance.
- **Reduced localization costs:** just by limiting vocabulary and reducing word count, companies can save 20% or more on localization costs.

Implementing controlled language is not trivial. When you transition to controlled language, you need to be thoughtful, proactive, and prepared for the long term. Rather than re-invent the wheel, start with the controlled language initiative that most closely matches your needs[17]:

- **Plain Language:** a US government regulation to provide clear communication in government documents. (plainlanguage.gov)
- **Simplified Technical English:** a specification originally developed for the aerospace industry (but now used in many regulated industries) that strictly limits vocabulary and syntax. (asd-ste100.org)
- **Caterpillar Fundamental English:** a vocabulary of about 850 words. Developed in the 1970s, it helped lay the foundation for controlled language.

Controlled language benefits your content strategy by maximizing consistency and reuse, improving efficiency, reducing localization costs, and improving quality control[14].

Pam Estes Brewer
Glossary

What is it?

Alphabetical list of terms and definitions that is used consistently by all stakeholders of a specific project or product, including localization.

Why is it important?

Glossaries support localization efforts by eliminating ambiguity in how terms are used in specific contexts, which, in turn, improves communication and translation. Glossaries intended for internal use or by the localization vendor tend to be more detailed than those intended for customers.

About Pam Estes Brewer

Dr. Pam Estes Brewer is a technical communicator, educator, and management consultant. She teaches in Mercer University's School of Engineering. She researches remote teaming, and her book entitled *International Virtual Teams: Engineering Global Success* [43] was published in 2015. She is a Certified Online Training Professional, a Fellow in the Society for Technical Communication, and an Associate Editor for *IEEE Transactions on Professional Communication.*

Email	brewer_pe@mercer.edu
Twitter	@brewerpe
LinkedIn	linkedin.com/in/pamestesbrewer

Why does a business professional need to know this?

Glossaries help to ensure that all stakeholders in a given project or product can share information effectively. To be effective in culturally specific contexts, glossaries should be created collaboratively with product and localization professionals.

Generally, glossaries play these important roles:

- ensure a consistent use of terms by people and electronic systems
- provide definitions of terms most important to a subject, product, or project
- account for the cultural context in which words are being used

In creating the glossary term and definition, you must consider how local application could affect that definition.

Words included in a glossary vary based on project need and are likely to include technical terms, project-proprietary terms, and other, more general, terms that might be easily misinterpreted.

For localization, an effective glossary definition needs additional details:

- parts of speech
- definitions expressed in the words and syntax that will be most easily understood by the intended audience(s)
- the context in which the definition applies
- an example of usage
- preferred term in each target language

Depending on the audience and purpose of a glossary, it could be published in a variety of formats and media. Localization experts should be familiar with several types of glossaries including term bases and published glossaries that are delivered to end users.

Glossaries and term bases are related, but not identical. Term bases are comprehensive for the company or product line, and typically contain more detail about the term than the glossary does. Term bases are usually intended for internal use by the content development and localization teams[41] [42].

Laura Creekmore
Metadata

What is it?
Attributes of content you can use to structure, semantically define, and target content.

Why is it important?
Extends the capabilities of content, making it more powerful and enabling efficient operation in a data-driven world.

About Laura Creekmore
Laura Creekmore and her company, Creek Content, help organizations end content chaos and communicate effectively, developing content strategy and information architecture for organizations in healthcare and other complex fields. Creekmore teaches content strategy as an adjunct faculty member at Kent State University.

Email	laura@creekcontent.com
Website	creekcontent.com
Twitter	@lauracreekmore
LinkedIn	linkedin.com/in/lauracreekmore

Why does a business professional need to know this?

Metadata can take many forms. In simplest terms, metadata describes attributes or constraints of a content field. Metadata provides additional context or information that tells software how to handle content. Metadata should be used in conjunction with business rules to deploy and design content appropriately.

Content may relate to one or more subjects, and you can use metadata to show those relationships. Many digital systems encode display information into metadata, but this creates confusion. You might be tempted to tag a video as "featured," but at best, "featured" is a temporary designation. Instead, use dates, times, subjects, content types, and constraints as metadata, and build display and presentation rules that use that metadata.

Though many organizations create their own customized metadata, using a metadata standard such as Dublin Core[84] (or an industry-specific standard) can simplify your work and make your content more extensible. Using a standard schema for metadata allows you to make your data interoperable with other industry-standard systems and can aid translation and localization efforts.

When your system serves multiple languages, cultures, or countries, ensure that you have considered how to translate metadata as well as content. Are the classifications the same in multiple countries? Sometimes differences in concepts, customs, and regulations are just as important to localization as the language, and these differences often show up in metadata.

Metadata is sometimes revealed to users (in faceted search, for instance), but most often, it's the behind-the-scenes workhorse that makes your life easier.

Stephanie Piehl
Term Extraction

What is it?

The analysis of a given text or *corpus*, with the goal of identifying relevant term candidates within their context. Also called *term mining* or *term harvesting*.

Why is it important?

Term extraction is the starting point of all terminology management tasks. Term extraction is usually followed by the elimination of inconsistencies. Well-managed terminology improves quality, reduces costs, and improves time to market.

About Stephanie Piehl

With Stephanie Piehl's passion for languages and cultures, it was only natural that she graduated in Applied Linguistic and Cultural Studies at the renowned FTSK in Germersheim, Germany. She brings over 10 years of experience in localization. Working as a localization coordinator on both the vendor and the client side, as a freelance translator, and now as an in-house terminologist at Agilent Technologies, Stephanie has gained insights of the industry from every perspective.

Email   stephanie.piehl7@agilent.com
LinkedIn   linkedin.com/in/stephanie-piehl-5a7a7730/

Why does a business professional need to know this?

When you extract terms, you are not only working on terminology, you are also managing the organization-specific or industry-specific knowledge. Terminology promotes knowledge sharing between people working in the same business field.

If you aim to improve the quality and consistency of your publications, term extraction is probably the best approach. When you start term extraction, you might find various synonyms and spelling variants for the same thing. For example, you might discover the terms electronic catalog, E-catalog, and eCatalog used as synonyms. Once you have identified synonyms and variants, you can determine which version of these terms should be used in all publications across all functional areas[129].

To start a term extraction task, compile a corpus from which you can extract term candidates. These term candidates are then validated and automatically or semi-automatically recorded. Usually, term extraction is either monolingual, to extract term candidates, or bilingual, to identify term candidates together with their equivalents in the *target language*.

Several tools exist that can help you to automate term extraction. Each tool has strengths and weaknesses, so there is no one-size-fits-all solution. Before you decide on a term extraction tool, test and evaluate the various tools[130].

In general, these tools use three main approaches:

- **Linguistic**: the tool searches the corpus for word combinations that match a certain morphological or syntactical pattern, for example adjective+noun.
- **Statistical**: the tool identifies repeated sequences of lexical items.
- **Hybrid**: a combination of the previous two approaches, and thus also the most frequently used approach.

Rebecca Schneider
Terminology Management

What is it?

The practice of proactively maintaining dictionaries and glossaries to improve consistency within an organization. Terms are organized and controlled based on accepted standards, with a clear set of guidelines dictating their use within local contexts.

Why is it important?

Terminology management enables correct and consistent use of terms throughout the writing or translation process, or any other effort requiring accurate vocabulary usage.

About Rebecca Schneider

Rebecca Schneider's career includes involvement in content strategy, library science, and knowledge management. In 2010, she formed Azzard Consulting, a content strategy services and staffing firm, based on the conviction that there are good, better, and best ways to manage content. She continues and builds on that work with AvenueCX. Rebecca has guided content strategy in a variety of industries, including automotive, semiconductors, telecommunications, retail, financial services, and international development.

Email	rschneider@avenuecx.com
Website	avenuecx.com
Twitter	@1MoreRebecca
LinkedIn	linkedin.com/in/rebeccaschneider/

Why does a business professional need to know this?

Words (or phrases) describe products or services; explain a product's mechanisms; or tell customers how to use a product. Such terms are also used to tag content to support activities such as reporting, search, and personalization.

Technical terms are incorporated into the lexicon based on usage in a variety of content types, including product sheets, material declarations, support articles, informational videos, etc. The governance committee works with content and localization teams to select terms that reflect the organization's perspective or that of a specific business unit and geographical region. Inconsistent use of terminology can cause confusion or result in legal problems, and, in particularly egregious medically related cases, it can kill[132] [133].

Advantages to carefully controlling terminology include:

- consistency of voice and tone
- linguistic quality
- uniform word usage across an entire organization (including company-specific terms)
- conformance to legal requirements in particular regions or countries
- protection of trademarked and registered product names

Careful terminology management can facilitate translation reuse, reduce errors during authoring or translation, shorten revision time, and help streamline the content creation and localization process.

Terminology management systems maintain terms in a central database and allow terminologists to organize approved (and unapproved) terms in multiple languages. These systems define terms and provide editorial guidelines based on pre-established rules.

Governance committees of editors, terminologists, localization experts, and in-country reviewers should define these rules and provide input into usage guidelines. Governance over terms is based both on systematic rules and on this committee's decisions[131].

 **Marketing**

Miguel Sepulveda
Context

What is it?

The parts of written or spoken text surrounding a piece of content that clarify the meaning, and which are particularly important when multiple meanings could be attributed to that content.

Why is it important?

When multiple meanings are possible, translators need background and reference information so they can choose the right word. Having context available is crucial for localizers to provide a top-notch translation.

About Miguel Sepulveda

Miguel Sepulveda is a computer engineer with a QA background (British Computer Society). He is certified in Project Management (PMP) and holds a Master's degree in HR. In 1995, he entered the localization industry, working for Microsoft as a Spanish specialist. He is passionate about public speaking (CC member of Toastmasters International) and a video games/localization freak. Both things merged in his work as a localization manager for EA and King. He is part of the advisory board for LocWorld (GLRT).

Email	Miguel.Sepulveda@king.com
Website	yolocalizo.com
Twitter	@yolocalizo
LinkedIn	linkedin.com/in/miguels1/

Why does a business professional need to know this?

Often, it is wrongly assumed that all translations are done in context. However, in many situations, a translator receives just the snippet of text being translated.

For example, consider a file that contains text exported from a mobile app, but the translator doesn't have access to the app. Without that context, how would the translator know how to translate the word *Home*? Does it refer to a house? Or does it refer to a Home Page?

And what about *Table*? Are we referring to an array of data or a piece of furniture?

In January 1996, Microsoft's Bill Gates said, "Content is King." Two decades later the King has a partner, because today, context is the Queen!

Why is context the Queen in the localization industry?

Context is crucial for a top-notch translation. However, translators do not always receive precise instructions or a *localization kit* to support them in their translations endeavors.

Here are three recommendations to provide meaningful context to translators:

- Add screenshots and/or an explanation next to the *source* text to be translated.
- Use a descriptive key name. For example, "FB_Connect_Error" is more intuitive than just "Error."
- Create a database, form, or forum to share ideas (a Google Doc, on-line database, etc.) and facilitate the dialog between translators and clients. Providing a way for the teams to interact can minimize embarrassing mistakes.

Next time someone asks why context is important, consider the poor translator trying to guess whether "fly" is an insect or a verb[13].

Laura Di Tullio
Ethnography

What is it?
A systematic method used to perform qualitative research aimed at understanding cultures, groups, and organizations.

Why is it important?
Ethnography has evolved, spanning across several anthropology specialties, and ethnographers have joined forces with communication science and market research practitioners. The discipline has moved away from rigorous academia toward a more pragmatic and fast-paced approach. Some large corporations use ethnographers for market research, but the potential of ethnography is still largely overlooked[24].

About Laura Di Tullio
Laura Di Tullio has worked in Italy, France, Belgium, and the U.S., gaining international experience and acquiring knowledge of different cultures. She currently works in cross-cultural training and terminology management for clients, including large multinational corporations. She holds Master's degrees in Terminology Management and in Translation and a BA in Applied Foreign Languages. She presents at various conferences on the topics of effective communication across cultures and of terminology management.

Email   lditullio30@hotmail.com
LinkedIn   linkedin.com/in/laura-di-tullio-4b0692/

Why does a business professional need to know this?

Ethnography provides a structured methodology for understanding and interpreting the cultural constructs in which people live.

In corporate environments, ethnography can inform market research, user experience design, global usability testing, persona development, and audience analysis. In these cases, companies look for contradictions between what their customers declare they do and how they really act, so they can identify their customers' hidden needs. What people say, what people do, and what people say they do don't always align, and this misalignment can expose needs or barriers that a product or service could resolve.

In addition, cultural differences can cause people to perceive or interact with a product or service differently than expected. In his work for IBM on cultural dimensions, Geert Hofstede attempted to define and model these behaviors[20]. Others have since built on this work[21] [25].

Despite concerns that corporate ethnographic research lacks rigor, such research can inform not only the design and development of new products and services, but also allow the discovery and investigation of new markets. Companies such as Intel have interpreted their customers' needs and adjusted their strategies accordingly, for instance, by creating new business units.

Ethnography can provide these insights:

- Ensure that content resonates with the audience and translates well.
- Avoid cultural blunders[26].
- Adjust culture-bound metaphors and images.
- Choose whether or not to translate product names, slogans, ads, etc.
- Avoid costly errors or unnecessary rebranding.

Used well, ethnography can improve a company's globalization efforts and give it an advantage in the global market[22] [23].

Esther Curiel
Primary Market

What is it?

The market segment that a company considers to be the most important to their objectives and, therefore, their main focus.

Why is it important?

Companies segment their markets to help them devise the most effective go-to-market strategy for each segment. Content and localization strategies will be different for primary, secondary, and tertiary markets.

About Esther Curiel

Esther Curiel is a program manager and global content quality strategist at Vistatec. She has been helping brands create great user experiences across global markets for over 15 years. Lately, her interest has been focused on integrating developments from the content marketing world into localization processes. Esther believes that by collaborating more closely together, localization and marketing can help brands achieve international growth objectives much more effectively. Her mission is to facilitate such collaboration.

Email	esthercuriel28@gmail.com
Website	vistatec.com
Twitter	@esther_curiel
LinkedIn	linkedin.com/in/esther-curiel-60a07a16/

Why does a business professional need to know this?

Primary markets (which typically, although not always, translate as Tier-1 languages in localization) benefit from higher budgets, the ability to localize more content, and in-country staff that localization teams ideally can collaborate with to discuss terminology, develop style guides, and fine-tune the messaging for higher impact with the target audience.

Target market segmentation requires a very good understanding of customer needs, pain points, and priorities[102]. Localizers armed with information on the customer personas that the content was created for, the needs that the content is trying to address, and the strategy that will be used to ensure it reaches its audience, are better placed to deliver quality localized content that will help the brand achieve its goals. If the content requires *transcreation* or when creating original content for different languages, customer and market information becomes even more important.

In addition, localization, marketing, and in-country teams can collaborate to decide how to address potential differences in the content required for each primary market, including:

- **Customer personas:** for example, differences in income level, age, or level of seniority[101].
- **Culture:** for example, differences in payment methods or the structure of online forms.
- **Regulatory/legal:** for example, differences in regulations for email marketing in Europe vs. the US (Europe requires active consent (opt in), the US doesn't).
- **Relevance:** for example, it is better to re-create customer testimonials using customers from each target market, rather than translating from the primary market (unless the customer is well known in the target markets)[103].

Carmen Avilés Suárez
Simship

What is it?

The concurrent distribution of all content related to a particular product or service to all target markets in the appropriate languages. Also known as *Simultaneous Shipment*.

Why is it important?

Releasing a product in all markets at the same time helps ensure successful product introductions, stronger sales, and greater customer satisfaction[112].

About Carmen Avilés Suárez

Carmen Avilés Suárez's passion for languages, cultures, and science brought her to explore new areas and moved her from a BS in molecular biology to the localization industry 10 years ago. Her current interests range from content strategy, cultural adaptation, and multicultural communications to localization process optimization. Outside work, she enjoys spending time with her multicultural family and rescued dogs out in nature and cooking.

Email   carmen.aviles@agilent.com
LinkedIn   linkedin.com/in/carmen-avilés-suárez-6274a823/

Why does a business professional need to know this?

The concept of simship is currently applied not only to software, but also to digital content.

Releasing multilingual content simultaneously in all markets requires a well-structured and clear *globalization* strategy that incorporates a global content strategy, which then informs the localization strategy. Too often, the localization teams are asked for a localization strategy without having the other two defined.

- **Globalization strategy:** addresses how the organization ensures that its business processes support customers outside of its home market.
- **Global content strategy:** focuses on the processes, structures, and relationships for all the content the company produces.
- **Global localization strategy:** focuses on how the company decides which content needs to be localized or adapted, and how much content is required to enable audiences in local markets to experience the same quality of customer journey as that enjoyed in the source locale.

Localization teams use the localization strategy to decide where, what, and how much content to localize, based on how much content has been created for the source locale.

Understanding the globalization and content strategy – how content is developed and managed – helps the team ensure that localization processes are scalable, support the strategy, and can deliver on simship promises.

Managing content in an *Agile environment* can help decrease turnaround times while maintaining quality as simship becomes the new normal[113]. Automation is a key piece of this success, because it allows teams to quickly deliver localized content based on market expectations[114] [115].

Patrick Nunes
Transcreation

What is it?

The process of re-developing or adapting content from one culture to another, while transferring its meaning and maintaining its intent, style, and voice.

Why is it important?

In transcreation, the concepts, feelings, and call to action that are expressed in the *source* are maintained in the *target*, but the emphasis, design, and the text are oriented specifically to the target culture. While there are some grey areas, transcreation goes much deeper than localization typically does and, consequently, incurs significantly higher costs.

About Patrick Nunes

As the Global Communications Manager at Rotary International, Patrick Nunes is passionate about the development and implementation of transcultural communication strategies to advance strategic initiatives and grow global brand presence. He firmly believes in the concept of re-branding the role of linguists in order to ensure that localization is not an afterthought, but a crucial component of global business planning and product lifecycle.

Email	patrick.nunes@rotary.org
Website	rotary.org
Twitter	@patricknunes
LinkedIn	linkedin.com/in/patricknunes/

Why does a business professional need to know this?

The concept of transcreation is relatively new. Although transcreation is often referred to as a process for marketing content, you can transcreate many types of message.

Essentially a content creation process, transcreation requires skills that go beyond language and culture, such as the capacity to relate to the target audience and to create content that establishes trust and motivates the audience to take action. Transcreation often depends less on the source text than traditional translation because each regional version might require the creation of new images, storylines, and copy.

Successful transcreation must be an integral part of the content creation process, not an afterthought. It requires the following elements:

- knowledge of the intent, messaging, tone, and style to be conveyed (e.g., a creative brief or regulatory summary)
- deep understanding of the target market's culture, idioms, and preferences
- budget and schedule to support the task in all the markets where it is needed

It is crucial that the transcreation teams truly understand the concept and emotional intent of the message so that they can successfully transfer the intent globally. Transcreation is not something to be rushed through; all the right elements must be created to support the full intent of the message[136].

Because translation, localization, and transcreation are separate but related processes, it is important to be aware of when to apply which process to what type of content. In addition, the transcreation of branding and marketing content should always be tested and vetted in every market where it will be used[137] [138] [139].

 **Standards**

Felix Sasaki
Internationalization Tag Set (ITS)

What is it?
A W3C (World Wide Web Consortium) standard that provides concepts for the automated creation and processing of multilingual web content.

Why is it important?
With ITS, processes can be automated with standardized metadata called ITS data categories. Example processes include translation package creation, *machine translation*, and quality review.

About Felix Sasaki
Felix Sasaki joined the W3C in 2005 and worked in the Internationalization Activity until March 2009. In 2012, he rejoined the W3C team as a Fellow on behalf of DFKI (German Research Center for Artificial Intelligence). He was co-chair of the Multilingual Web-LT Working Group and co-editor of the Internationalization Tag Set (ITS) 2.0 specification. His main field of interest is the application of Web technologies for representation and processing of multilingual information.

Email	felix@sasakiatcf.com
Twitter	@fsasaki
LinkedIn	linkedin.com/in/felixsasaki

Why does a business professional need to know this?

ITS saves time, increases quality, and allows for automation and other ways to process multilingual content. Because ITS makes it easier for localization tools to work with information in source content, using it can save time and expense, for example, when integrating with content production tools (CMS, XML tools, etc.).

ITS provides data categories such as Translate, Terminology, or Elements within Text, which help to configure *machine translation (MT)* pre-processing, post-processing, or the MT engine itself. These categories can improve quality.

New application scenarios are also possible. For example, the Text Analytics data category allows you to annotate content with lexical or conceptual information.

In this way, the localization specialist becomes a content enrichment architect and localized content gets additional value, for example, with marketing departments and for search engine optimization.

A key aspect of ITS is that the ITS data categories are available, at least partially, in standard content formats such as *DITA*, *DocBook*, and HTML5 and in the upcoming *XLIFF 2.1* standard for localization interchange. Because these categories are already familiar, it is easier to learn the new uses of the ITS. In addition, out-of-the-box tool support is growing for both open source solutions and commercial products[61].

Gábor Ugray
Interoperability

What is it?

The ability of different systems to exchange and make use of information (e.g., each other's data formats) and to work together, often in real time.

Why is it important?

Localization is a complex process that requires many different components to interact smoothly. When selecting tools, make sure that interoperability is included as a feature.

About Gábor Ugray

Gábor Ugray is co-founder of Kilgray, creators of the memoQ collaborative translation environment and translation management system. He is now Kilgray's Head of Innovation, and when he's not busy building MVPs, he blogs at jealousmarkup.xyz and tweets as @twilliability.

Email	gabor.ugray@kilgray.com
Website	kilgray.com
Twitter	@twilliability

Why does a business professional need to know this?

Each step in the localization process requires extracting or importing content from one application into another. When localization vendors analyze a client's files, part of their analysis involves determining how easily the content transfers from the source application into the translation tool and back. When clients want to change vendors, they need to be able to export their *translation memories (TM)* from one tool and import them into another. Problems with either export or import can quickly break the localization budget.

Therefore, each tool in the localization solution must not only be the best one for the job, it must also work seamlessly with all the other tools to ensure that employees are at their most productive and that the business enjoys maximum *return on investment (ROI)*. Interoperability is what allows these tools to work together.

In the past, interoperability mostly focused on file formats, such as *TMX* or *XLIFF* [63], but as most software moves into the cloud, a new challenge is to ensure that cloud services work together seamlessly (or at all) through their *APIs*.

Failing to prioritize interoperability could leave your business with a set of siloed systems and a lot of wasteful and repetitive manual work to operate the localization process end-to-end.

Rodolfo M. Raya
SRX

What is it?

Segmentation Rules eXchange. An open XML-based standard that describes how translation and other language-processing tools should split text fragments for processing.

Why is it important?

SRX helps in achieving better translation reuse at the sentence level from *translation memory (TM)* engines.

About Rodolfo M. Raya

Rodolfo M. Raya is Chief Technical Officer at Maxprograms, where he develops multi-platform translation/localization and content publishing tools using XML and Java technology.

Email   rmraya@maxprograms.com
Website   maxprograms.com
LinkedIn   linkedin.com/in/rodolfo-m-raya-761939a

Why does a business professional need to know this?

Translation memory (TM) is a technology that reduces localization costs by reusing previous translations. TM benefits are usually larger when working with sentences instead of paragraphs. Different tools split paragraphs into sentences in different ways when using their default settings. SRX was created by LISA (Localization Industry Standards Association) to standardize the rules used to segment text.

Understanding how tools break large texts into smaller pieces is important for maximizing the reuse of TM assets when using multiple translation tools.

SRX knowledge is useful when working with text that includes specialized abbreviations that localization tools don't contemplate in their default configurations. Adjusting the rules according to the text produces more legible segments and enhances TM *leveraging* at a later stage.

SRX rules use regular expressions to indicate where to break text and what exceptions should be considered. The regular expressions used in SRX are defined in the specification document, which includes an appendix that contains examples[119] [121].

The SRX standard definition and XML schema are currently available at the Globalization and Localization Association (GALA) web site[44].

Christian Taube
TMX

What is it?

Translation Memory Exchange. An XML-based standard that facilitates the exchange of data between different *translation memory (TM)* tools.

Why is it important?

The capability of moving data between different tools makes TMX important to the industry. However, its flexibility can limit its applicability, because tool vendors often create variants, which can hinder interoperability.

About Christian Taube

Christian Taube is Chief Solutions Officer at Xplanation. He has worked in the localization industry since 1997 in various roles as a project manager, technology lead, and consultant. He co-founded two localization start-ups. With IT industry experience since 1990, he has also gained experience in translation, technical writing, system administration, and development team leadership.

Email	christian.taube@xplanation.com
Website	xplanation.com
Twitter	@ctaube2011
LinkedIn	linkedin.com/in/christiantaube/

Why does a business professional need to know this?

If a company using a *computer-aided translation (CAT)* tool decides to start using a new or different tool, for a number of reasons, they need to move their valuable translation memories from the old tool into the new one. TMX (Translation Memory eXchange) enables that migration. All CAT tools can make use of TMX files and export the translation memories contained in the CAT to a TMX file. This is the strength of the standard.

TMX was initially released in 1997. The most recent version is 1.4b, released in 2005[134]. The standard has not been substantially updated since, although some work was done on a 2.0 version that, as of the date this was written, has not been completed.

Tool vendors are free to decide how they implement the standard. There are no rules about how to extract text segments and inline markup, such as bold, italic, etc., into a translatable document. So, software vendors often create different flavors of tags for storing these elements in a TMX file because they have different architectural goals. Thus, migrating data from one tool to another almost always leads to a loss of *leverage* in the match results, despite both tools being able to create completely valid TMX that complies with the standard. This is the standard's weakness and makes it hard to apply in everyday situations.

It is important to understand that TMX is not the same as *XLIFF*. The latter enables the exchange of *bitext* data specifically for translation, while TMX is specifically for the exchange of full TMs.

Ken Lunde
Unicode

What is it?

A character encoding standard that provides a cross-platform, uniform, and robust digital representation of the scripts for the world's languages.

Why is it important?

Unicode has become the de facto way in which characters for the scripts of the world's languages are represented in modern digital devices, meaning that Unicode is a prerequisite for all digital text.

About Ken Lunde

Dr. Ken Lunde has worked at Adobe for over 25 years, specializing in CJKV Type Development. He architected the open source *Source Han Sans* and *Source Han Serif* Pan-CJK typeface families that were released in 2014 and 2017, respectively. He is the author of *CJKV Information Processing* [150] and also regularly publishes articles to Adobe's *CJK Type Blog*.

Email   lunde@adobe.com
Website   blogs.adobe.com/CCJKType/
Twitter   @ken_lunde
LinkedIn linkedin.com/in/kenlunde/
Facebook facebook.com/ken.lunde

Why does a business professional need to know this?

Unicode[143] provides the foundation for anything related to text data. The Unicode standard is developed and maintained by the Unicode Consortium. The uniform representation for all of Unicode's 136,690 characters – as of Version 10.0, released on June 20, 2017 – helps to ensure interoperability and translatability of any text-related tasks that you might encounter, whether it is for multilingual user interface (UI) strings or translations of entire manuals[146].

Any implementation that handles text but does not support Unicode is a completely wasted effort, because its text data cannot easily interoperate with Unicode-based implementations that are now commonplace (see the Unicode FAQ[145]).

It is important to understand that Unicode is much more than a huge bucket of characters covering 139 scripts that are used by an even larger number of the world's languages (including Egyptian hieroglyphics):

- Unicode defines several properties that determine how its characters are to behave.
- The UCD (*Unicode Character Database*)[149] is the primary source for these properties, which are documented in UAX #44[144]. Some of the properties include line breaking, casing, bidirectionality, inherent width, and so on.

Closely related to Unicode are the following two important and useful projects:

- ICU (*International Components for Unicode*)[148], which provides robust libraries that implement many functions for properly handling Unicode-based text data according to the UCD.
- CLDR (*Common Locale Data Repository*)[147], which provides an enormous amount of locale data that are used by an increasingly large number of OSes and apps.

Both projects are frequently updated, and Unicode itself is now on an annual release cycle.

David Filip
XLIFF

What is it?

XML Localization Interchange File Format. The only open standard *bitext* format. This is how *computer-aided translation (CAT)* tools can be interoperable.

Why is it important?

XLIFF is important because managing bitext is the core process in localization. XLIFF keeps source and target aligned throughout all transformations in the roundtrip through the localization process, which should be standards-based, not proprietary.

About David Filip

David Filip is chair (Convener) of the OASIS XLIFF OMOS Technical Committee (TC); secretary, lead editor, and liaison officer of the OASIS XLIFF TC; former co-chair and editor of W3C ITS 2.0; Advisory Editorial Board member for *MultiLingual* magazine; and co-chair of the JIAMCATT Standards IG. David works as a research fellow at the ADAPT Centre, Trinity College Dublin, Ireland. Before 2011, he oversaw key research and change projects for Moravia and held research scholarships at universities in Vienna, Hamburg, and Geneva. He holds a PhD in Analytic Philosophy (2004) from Masaryk University.

Email	david.filip@adaptcentre.ie
Website	adaptcentre.ie/team-members/person-detail/david-filip
Twitter	@merzbauer
LinkedIn	linkedin.com/in/davidfatdavidf/

Why does a business professional need to know this?

Professional, industry-scale localization and translation services must use bitext, which keeps the *segments* (typically sentences) and logical units (typically paragraphs) in the *source language* aligned with those in the *target language* [155].

While the industry has been using proprietary bitext formats, proprietary formats cause lack of interoperability and vendor lock-in. Because XLIFF is an open standard bitext format, it prevents this problem.

Imagine a professional reviewer doing quality assurance (QA) for a translation without having access to the source. Even if the source can be located, the reviewer would still need to manually parse and re-parse the unaligned and disconnected source and target. Clearly, this is not scalable.

XLIFF 2 Core[151] is designed to facilitate the round trip from extracting source content to merging target content back into the environment. XLIFF modules provide interoperable metadata, enhancing specialized collaboration and automation, including terminology or *translation memory (TM)* matches.

XLIFF 2.0 replaced XLIFF 1.2[153] in 2014. Albeit widely adopted, XLIFF 1.2 was both too big (many features, yet no modularity) and terrifyingly slim (lack of specificity), which allowed for mutually incompatible implementations.

XLIFF 2.1[152] will supersede XLIFF 2.0 in 2017. It adds advanced validation capability and an *internationalization tag set (ITS)* module that brings full native support for ITS 2.0. Advanced validation capability from 2.1 can be used to validate both XLIFF 2.1 and XLIFF 2.0 documents more comprehensively. XLIFF 2.1 is backward compatible with XLIFF 2.0, thanks to the modular architecture of XLIFF 2[156] [157].

Alessandra Binazzi
Glossary of Business Terms

At its core, the primary benefit of localization is to facilitate global business development and communication. Localization is an often unseen cost of doing business on a global scale, and yet, businesses would fail without it.

As a result, many terms common to general business and marketing are important to localization as well. This glossary contains a selection of business-related terms that are referenced in this book.

About Alessandra Binazzi

Alessandra Binazzi Consulting develops localization programs tailored to needs of organizations at the early stages of a multilingual strategy. Alessandra is a 20-year, multilingual professional with a varied experience and one common thread: international markets and customers. University educated in Boston, she was exposed to global technology companies from the beginning of her career, with a focus on multilingual digital content.

Email   alessandra@binazziconsulting.com

business intelligence (BI)

A technology-driven process for analyzing data and presenting it in a meaningful way. The goal of BI is to enable management to make informed business decisions. In localization, BI focuses on analyzing internal data on quality, turn-around time, and process in order to optimize these elements. External data analysis focuses on local customer experience and satisfaction.

crowdsourcing

Sourcing model that uses a large number of participants from a community (online or other) to complete a particular task. This method can use volunteers or paid participants. In localization, this model is often used by organizations that have access to large pools of loyal multilingual users.

games localization

The process of making games (usually electronic ones) acceptable to a particular locale. This process includes translating the written and audio content and localizing the visual and cultural content.

gamification

Methodology using game techniques and elements to engage users and customers in a business process or marketing activity. In localization, gamification is used most frequently to engage linguists in a crowdsourcing model.

localization kit

A checklist provided to a language services provider (LSP) when submitting a localization project request. The localization kit enables the LSP to produce an appropriate cost estimate and project plan. The localization kit also contains specifications, a list of all source files (content, graphics, resource files, metadata, etc.), template files, and a list of authoring and software development tools used.

market

A physical or nominal place where buyers and sellers interact and, therefore, is driven by the forces of demand and supply. A market is often defined by a certain locale or region. In localization, supply includes translators, localization service providers (LSPs), technology companies, service companies, etc. Demand includes any organization that needs localization services, which potentially includes nearly all existing organizations.

persona

A fictional character created to represent a particular type of customer or user. Personas can assist in identifying ways that someone might use the product or service.

project management

The discipline of starting, planning, completing, controlling, and closing a set of tasks to achieve specific goals and meet specific criteria. In localization, steps can include sourcing linguists, processing requests, assigning work to appropriate resources, scheduling work, ensuring quality checks, and delivering translated content.

return on investment (ROI)

The result (monetary or otherwise) generated as a direct outcome of a particular investment. In localization, ROI is used to assess the value of investment in new tools, new languages, new translation service, etc. The formula `Return-Costs = ROI` returns an absolute value; the formula `Return/Cost = ROI` returns a percentage value for comparing investments.

social games

Games played online in a group that require players to interact with both the game elements and other people. Such games can be complex to localize because of their interactivity and contextual nature.

strategy

A high-level plan for achieving one or more goals. A strategy usually covers a long period of time. A localization strategy identifies what resources, tools, and processes are required to deliver high quality, timely products to local markets in the local language.

user experience (UX)

Overall involvement that a user/customer has when interacting with a product, service, or content. It includes both the practical and emotional experience of the user. In localization, the focus is put on users in the local market and their interaction with the localized product, service, or content.

workflow

The sequence of steps/tasks through which a project passes from start to completion. Workflows make up a process. In localization, a typical workflow is the series of task from submission of a translation request, through the translation process (file management, deployment to language resources, translation, review, QA, etc.) to delivery of translated files and deployment of the translated content.

Madison Van Doren
Glossary of Linguistics Terms

Effective localization depends on linguistic competence in multiple languages. The terms in this glossary are provided to assist non-linguists in understanding concepts related to the language aspects of localization and translation.

The definitions of the alphabetic, logographic, segmental, and syllabic writing systems were adapted from the work of Erik Vogt, who wrote the essay for the term *script*.

About Madison Van Doren

Madison Van Doren is a recent graduate of Colorado State University with a Bachelor's degree in English with a concentration in Language and a minor in Linguistics. She is pursuing an MA in Linguistics at Queen Mary University of London with research interests in historical and sociolinguistics.

Email   madisonvandoren@gmail.com
LinkedIn   linkedin.com/in/madisonvandoren

Glossary of Linguistics Terms

accent mark

Writing conventions used to differentiate similar letters in a language to indicate linguistic clues, such as a change in pronunciation or verb conjugation. For example, in French, an accent mark marks a verb in the past participle such that *coupé* is the past participle and *coupe* is the first-person, singular, present tense. Similarly, an accent mark can identify a change in phonemes, such as the cedilla on *Ça* in French, which indicates that the "c" is pronounced with an /s/ sound instead of a /k/ sound.

alphabetic writing system

The writing system for a language in which there is a symbol for each consonant and vowel. Alphabets are also known as segmental systems. These systems combine a limited list of characters to represent spoken language. There is not a direct correlation, but letters are intended to indicate individual phonemes. This writing system is common in European languages; however, it can also be seen in other regions, such as Korea.

case

Grammatical case refers to the role a word plays in the structure of a sentence, such as the subject of the clause or object of the verb. Some languages change the form of a word (inflect) to indicate case, while other languages rely on word order. It is important to understand the difference between part of speech (nouns, verbs, etc.) and case (subject, object, etc.) because these are the foundation of syntax. Understanding the meaning of sentences and larger texts depends on understanding case.

character

A general term for a symbol in a writing system. In the alphabetic writing system used for English, a character is a letter, such as "a" or "s." In a syllabic writing system, such as Japanese hiragana, a character is one symbol that represents a consonant vowel pair. In a logographic writing system, such as Chinese hànzì, a character is a logogram representing a *morpheme* or a word.

corpus

A collection of spoken or written linguistic texts used to observe greater patterns in language. Uses include generating lists of words that are commonly used together or identifying vocabulary popular in a specific genre.

The Language of Localization

Cyrillic script

The characters used by most Slavic languages, including Russian, Bulgarian, and Serbian.

diacritical

The linguistic term for an *accent mark*. These marks indicate changes in pronunciation of a *phoneme*. The International Phonetic Alphabet (IPA) uses a standardized system of diacritical marks. The term diacritical is commonly used in academic literature.

gender

Grammatical gender differs from natural gender. Unlike English, which does not use grammatical gender, some languages assign nouns an arbitrary gender to categorize them. This affects how modifiers such as adjectives and articles are conjugated. This is common in Romance languages. Natural gender, meaning the sex of individuals, sometimes, but not always, matches the grammatical gender assigned to words. For example, the word for girl in Italian, *la ragazza*, is feminine in both grammatical and natural gender.

hànzì

The writing system of Chinese. The Chinese writing system is logographic, meaning that each character represents a whole *morpheme* or word. The hànzì characters have been borrowed by other Asian languages, including Japanese and Korean.

kanji

The Japanese writing system uses some characters borrowed from Chinese hànzì. These characters are used in combination with the other Japanese scripts such as katakana and hiragana. Although these characters are borrowed from Chinese, they don't always carry the same meanings in Japanese as they do in Chinese.

language family

Historical relationships between modern languages. Languages with common ancestry are grouped in linguistics as language families. This includes Romance languages, such as French and Spanish, which have Latin as a common ancestor, or Germanic languages such as Dutch, English, and German, which are descended from Proto-Germanic. Knowing the classifications of languages helps to explain how they relate to each other.

language

A communication system used by a group of people that assigns agreed upon meaning to arbitrary collections of sounds and symbols. To be a language, the system must be capable of communicating abstract concepts, such as emotions, and being used reflexively to talk about the language. These constraints are important for understanding how one person cannot invented a language alone because language depends on a communication exchange. Animal communication is also not considered language because abstract thought is limited.

Latin script

The characters common to most European languages, based on the Roman writing system used for Latin. It is descended from the Phoenician alphabet.

linguistics

The scientific study of language and its functions. Linguistics encompasses all aspects of human language from its history to the social implications. Research in linguistics provides modern information on language around the world and how best to understand complex topics, such as syntax or phonetics.

linguistic lead

The localization team member who is responsible for verifying the quality of the translation for a particular language. This person is typically more senior than the translators, has strong editing skills and domain knowledge, and has a clear picture of the translation goals and requirements. Linguistic leads provide guidance, answer questions, and help the project manager keep things on track.

logographic writing system

The oldest type of writing system, logographic writing systems use symbols that represent a complete word or *morpheme*. Chinese is an excellent example of a logographic script, but most languages also include logograms, such as numbers and the ampersand. Logographic characters don't indicate pronunciation. Therefore, multiple languages can use the same morphemes with different pronunciation. For example, Chinese, Japanese, and Korean share a large number of characters, but the pronunciation of most of these shared characters is different in each language.

matching penalty

Part of the algorithm used to determine whether or not a source *segment* is the same as one that already exists in the *translation memory*. To calculate the matching penalty, an algorithm can consider factors such as contextual cues, *fuzzy matches*, and whether a *pivot language* was used.

morpheme

The smallest meaningful unit in a language. Morphemes can be thought of as the building blocks of meaning and can be a standalone word or an affix – a prefix or suffix – that carries lexical or grammatical meaning. For example, the word *cat* is a morpheme in English because it has lexical meaning on its own and cannot be broken down into smaller pieces. The word *cats* has two morphemes, the lexical morpheme *cat* and the suffix *s*, which is a grammatical morpheme meaning plural.

neural machine translation (NMT)

An approach that uses an artificial neural network to determine matching and context. NMT systems progressively improve – and all parts of the system learn jointly – as they are exposed to more examples and content. They use a fraction of the memory that traditional statistical methods use. Google and Microsoft have adopted neural MT as their preferred methodology for machine translation. The Harvard NLP (*Natural Language Processing*) group has also developed an open source system called OpenNMT.

pivot language

An intermediary (and usually more common) language used to facilitate translation between two or more other languages. The pivot language (also known as a bridge language) is often, though not always, English. This is because English is the most common second language and the de facto language of global business, which means that a larger pool of trained translators know the combination of English and another language than other language combinations. For example, more translators know both English and Farsi than know both Farsi and Cherokee.

phoneme

Any sound that is used in a meaningful way by a specific language. The International Phonetic Alphabet lists all possible phonemes in human language and all humans are capable of making all phonemes. However, each language has a set number of phonemes. Therefore, people studying a new language can struggle to produce sounds that are not phonemic in their first language. For example, /i/ is the vowel in the English word beet and /ɪ/ is the vowel in bit. Both of these vowels are phonemes in English because they make a meaningful difference in a word. However, in Spanish, these sounds are not both phonemic because replacing one with the other does not change meaning. In Spanish, they are regarded as slight variations of the same sound.

romanji

A system of Japanese writing based on the Phoenician alphabet. Romanji uses Western writing, the same as English spelling, to transcribe the Japanese language. Romanji is commonly used to teach Westerners Japanese or to give examples of pronunciation, but it still follows the conventions of Japanese, including rules for when and how it is used.

segmental writing system

Usually alphabets. These systems use relatively few symbols that combine to form a range of phonemes and morphemes, representing spoken language. The meaning of the term *segmental* in linguistics differs from the meaning of *segments* in *translation memory*.

simplified Chinese

The writing system used in the People's Republic of China and other locales. Since the mid-20th century, the Chinese government has gradually simplified the Chinese characters, hànzì. They have reduced the number of characters commonly taught and used, and they have altered the way the characters are written.

syllabic writing system

A writing system in which characters represent syllables and are combined to indicate *morphemes*. Most commonly, syllabic writing systems only allow vowel (V) or consonant-vowel (CV) syllable structure. The Japanese kana (both hiragana and katakana) and Devanagari are examples of syllabic writing systems.

tense

The time to which a verb refers in a clause. Because language can communicate abstract thought, a verb can be inflected to indicate the time at which it took place. This includes past, present, and future tenses, as well as some more complex tenses like interior past. Other aspects of verbs, such as whether an action is complete or its duration, is not included in tense.

traditional Chinese

The writing system used in Taiwan and other locales. It represents original Chinese hànzì characters. The hànzì characters first appeared in the Han dynasty as a clerical script and are used by both Mandarin and Cantonese speakers, as well as speakers of other Chinese dialects.

vocabulary

A collection of words used by a group or individual for a specific purpose. Vocabulary can be specific, such as a list of scientific animal names, or it can refer to the full working vocabulary of an individual. The nuances of this term are important for translation, as well as for formulating relevant lists of terminology.

writing system

The conventions for writing in a language. The writing system of a language can indicate pronunciation, stress, syllable timing, or just lexical meaning. These systems can be classified into 3 general types. See *logographic*, *syllabic*, and *alphabetic* writing systems for more details.

Arle Lommel
Glossary of Standards Terms

Every industry follows particular standards and uses specific technologies and methodologies. The localization industry is no exception.

Standards bodies pull together experts from around the globe to ensure that their work represents current practices. The resulting standards encode best practices and help facilitate interoperability, information transfer, and process improvement.

The standards that are most integral to localization, including *Internationalization Tag Set*, *interoperability*, *SRX*, *TMX*, *Unicode*, and *XLIFF*, are described in detail in the main text and are not repeated here. This glossary highlights additional standards, technologies, and methodologies that are relevant to the localization industry. You can find a comprehensive list of translation and localization industry standards at GALA (Globalization and Localization Association)[44].

About Arle Lommel

Arle Lommel is a senior analyst with Common Sense Advisory (CSA Research), where he focuses on language technology and translation quality. A noted writer and speaker on localization and translation, he headed standards development at the Localization Industry Standards Association (LISA) and later at GALA, before working on translation quality topics at the German Research Center for Artificial Intelligence (DFKI). He has a PhD from Indiana University and currently resides in Bloomington, Indiana.

Email   arle.lommel@gmail.com
Website   commonsenseadvisory.com
Twitter   @ArleLommel
LinkedIn   linkedin.com/in/arlelommel/

accessibility

The ease with which a person can make use of a product, process, service, or content. In the context of localization, making a product accessible means eliminating barriers of language, usability, disability, and technology. Some of the standards and initiatives that govern accessibility include the Americans with Disabilities Act (USA)[45], Section 508 (USA)[46], Web Content Accessibility Guidelines (global)[47], Level Access (EU)[48], and ICTA Global (International Commission on Technology and Accessibility)[49].

Agile methodology

An iterative project management methodology that divides tasks into short phases of work (often called sprints), with frequent reassessment and adaptation. The originator of this method wrote a manifesto[50] to describe the principles. The manifesto forms the basis for several different Agile software methodologies, the most widespread being Scrum and Kanban. In the past few years, there has been a push to include localization in the Agile process.

application programming interface (API)

A specification that defines how software components interact and exchange data. APIs simplify automation of routine tasks. For example, a client can use an API to send content that is ready for translation from its content management system (CMS) directly and automatically to the localization vendor's project management system. In turn, the localization vendor can use an API to push translated content back into the client's CMS.

Bayesian spam filtering

A method that uses statistical analysis of an incoming email header and content to estimate the likelihood that it is spam. Bayesian spam filtering compares the frequency of the occurrence of particular words in an incoming message with the frequency of those words occurring in spam and legitimate email.

code page

A table of values used to map binary codes to textual characters, including some control characters. Today, most code pages have been superseded by Unicode, but legacy code pages still play an important role in many environments

DITA

Darwin Information Typing Architecture. An XML data model and architecture for authoring and publishing user documentation. It is an open standard that was developed by IBM and is now maintained by the OASIS DITA Technical Committee. Localization vendors need to understand the DITA architecture and unique file management requirements of processing DITA files for translation.

DocBook

An XML standard originally designed around a book model, DocBook has evolved to be useful for help systems, ebooks, and other forms of technical documentation. DocBook is widely used in the open source community. It is an open standard that was originally designed and implemented by HAL Computer Systems and O'Reilly and Associates, and is now maintained by the OASIS DocBook Technical Committee.

Dublin Core

An open organization that supports and promotes innovation and best practices in metadata design. The group maintains affiliations with several standards bodies and other metadata associations[84].

European Machinery Directive

Directive 2006/42/EC of the European Parliament and of the Council of 17 May 2006 governs safety in machinery placed on the market and mandates that safety notices must be in the local language. It also places requirements on the localization of some aspects of the user documentation.

faceted search

A technique for browsing or accessing information organized using semantic categories and multiple explicit dimensions, which allows the user to apply multiple filters. Amazon.com and many other websites use faceted search to narrow down search results by allowing you to search with particular categories (e.g., books, music, etc.).

ISO

The International Organization for Standardization coordinates the efforts of 150 countries to develop common standards for technology and products. These standards are intended to provide more efficient, safer, more consistent, and cleaner development practices (https://www.iso.org).

LISA OSCAR

A standards special interest group in the Localization Industry Standards Association (LISA). When LISA folded in 2011, its portfolio of standards was placed under a Creative Commons Attribution 3.0 license. These standards include: *TMX*, *TBX/ISO 30042*, and *SRX*. The GALA website provides links to these standards[51].

LISA QA model

A software tool and abstract model that was used for evaluating the quality of translated documents and user interfaces[52]. It provided a way to categorize and count errors in translated products to determine adherence to expectations. Widely implemented and modified, it remains highly influential, but has been supplanted by *Multidimensional Quality Metrics (MQM)*.

multidimensional quality metrics (MQM)

A framework for defining task-specific, translation-quality metrics, based on a shared vocabulary of error types[53]. It is currently in the standardization process in ASTM Committee F43 (American Society for Testing and Materials; now known as ASTM International). The DQF (Dynamic Quality Framework) Error Typology is a subset of MQM that has been widely adopted in the translation industry.

NSGCIS

National Standard Guide for Community Interpreting. This Canadian standard is used to certify localization service providers as community interpreters (https://tlolink.com/2fU6r6A).

OASIS

The Organization for the Advancement of Structured Information Standards (https://oasis-open.org). A global nonprofit consortium that works to develop and harmonize standards for computer- and Internet-related activities, particularly as they relate to data structure and exchange (e.g., security, Internet of Things, XLIFF, DITA, DocBook, etc.).

OAXAL

Open Architecture for XML Authoring and Localization. An OASIS initiative that combines various OASIS and OSCAR standards into an overarching architecture for XML authoring and localization.

Okapi Framework

An open source, cross-platform set of tools for localizing and translating content and software. The Okapi framework supports interoperability. You can download tools from the Okapi website: http://okapiframework.org/.

pattern matching

The process of checking a given sequence to identify recurring similarities. When enough similarities exist, they are flagged in the system as possible equivalents.

Quality Metric for Language Translation of Service Information (SAE J2450)

A standard that establishes quality metrics for translating automotive service information. The goal is to provide more objective measures of quality and to ensure that the translations are consistent and accurate, regardless of target language. The standard is available from the SAE website (http://standards.sae.org/j2450_201608/).

TAUS

Translation Automation User Society (https://taus.net). An organization that works to promote and improve machine translation by facilitating innovation, open platforms, and collaboration. This group develops standards, APIs, and other tools to support machine translation.

TermBase eXchange (TBX)

A standard (also known as ISO 30042) that provides an XML-based framework for representing structured terminology data. This framework facilitates interoperability of *terminology management systems* [54].

Translation Services—Requirements for Translation Services (ISO 17100)

A standard, based on the historic EN 15038 standard, that provides minimum qualification requirements for the human translation process involving quality and service delivery. It gives localization service providers (LSPs) guidelines for managing core processes, resources, and other activities involved in delivering a quality translation service. The standard is available for purchase from the ISO website[55].

W3C

World Wide Web Consortium (https://w3.org). This international community works to develop standards for the Web. It is led by Tim Berners-Lee and Dr. Jeffrey Jaffe. Working groups focus on different aspects of the Web, e.g., HTML5.

Web Content Accessibility Guidelines (WCAG)

A working group of the W3C that works to ensure that the Web is designed to work for all people, regardless of their locale and culture, as well as technological, physical, and mental limitations[47].

Web Ontology Languages (OWL)

A semantic web language created by the W3C that is designed to enable computers to understand the complex knowledge about things and relationships between things.

UTF-8 and UTF-16

Unicode Transformation Format. An algorithmic mapping of every Unicode code point to a unique byte sequence. Every UTF type supports lossless round-tripping. UTF-8 is most common on the Web. UTF-16 is used in Java and Windows. The number denotes the code unit size (8 bits or 16 bits in this case). Refer to the Unicode FAQ for more information[145].

XML

Extensible Markup Language. A standard developed by the World Wide Web Consortium (*W3C*) that defines rules for creating text-based languages that are both human- and machine-readable. XML is the basis for many localization standards, including *XLIFF*, *TMX*, and *TBX*, as well as content standards such as *DocBook* and *DITA*. XML markup allows great flexibility in designing and managing multilingual content.

References

Augmented Translation by Arle Lommel

[1] *Augmented Translation Powers up Language Services*
https://tlolink.com/2yiGd7F
DePalma, Don and Arle Lommel. (15 February 2017) Common Sense Advisory Research blog entry on augmented translation.

[2] *Augmented Translation Puts Translators Back in the Center*
https://tlolink.com/2hx3Sr3
Lommel, Arle. (19 May 2017) tekom blog entry on augmented translation.

Bitext by Aljoscha Burchardt

[3] *Parallel Text Alignment*
https://en.wikipedia.org/wiki/Parallel_text
Wikipedia article on parallel texts.

[4] *Bitext Word Alignment*
https://en.wikipedia.org/wiki/Bitext_word_alignment
Wikipedia article on bitext word alignment.

Character Encoding by Chase Tingley

[5] *W3C: Character Encodings for Beginners*
https://www.w3.org/International/questions/qa-what-is-encoding

[6] *W3C: Character Encodings: Essential Concepts*
https://www.w3.org/International/articles/definitions-characters/
A more in-depth discussion of characters, character encodings, and related concepts, with an emphasis on Unicode.

Character Set by Dave Ruane

[7] *Official Character set names on the internet (IANA)*
https://www.iana.org/assignments/character-sets/character-sets.xhtml

[8] *Programmer information on Character sets and encoding: What every programmer absolutely needs to know*
http://kunststube.net/encoding/

[9] *Unicode, UTF8 & Character Sets: The Ultimate Guide*
https://tlolink.com/2hxg7nB

[10] *Universal Character Set Characters*
https://tlolink.com/2xvplLc
Open standard that lists the Universal Character Set characters.

Computer-aided translation (CAT) by Jost Zetzsche

[11] *Computer-Aided Translation*
https://tlolink.com/2hx5y41
Garcia, Ignacio. In: *Routledge Encyclopedia of Translation Technology*.
Ed. Sin-Wai Chan. Routledge: Oxford/New York: 68-87.

[12] *A Translator's Tool Box for the 21st Century: A Computer Primer for Translators*
http://www.internationalwriters.com/toolbox/
Zetzsche, Jost. Winchester Bay: International Writers' Group. 2003-2017.

Context by Miguel Sepulveda

[13] *Context in Translating*
https://tlolink.com/2xmH1t1
Nida, Eugene Albert. Explains the different kinds of contexts that translators must consider.

Controlled Language by Katherine (Kit) Brown-Hoekstra

[14] *The Content Pool*
http://xmlpress.net/publications/the-content-pool
Porter, Alan. Porter's book provides a great overview of content strategy.
Pages 50-54 talk about controlled language in more detail.

[15] *Controlled Language: The Next Big Thing in Translation*
http://www.translationdirectory.com/articles/article1359.php
Muegge, Uwe. This article talks about the implications of controlled language for translation. Controlled language is part of terminology management.

[16] *The Benefits of Using Controlled Language*
https://www.gala-global.org/blog/benefits-using-controlled-language
Brown-Hoekstra, Kit. The essay for this book is based on this presentation and blog post for GALA.

[17] *Summary of Controlled Language Initiatives*
https://tlolink.com/2hx2KDQ

Culture by Katherine (Kit) Brown-Hoekstra

[18] *Intercultural Communication: A Contextual Approach, 7th ed.*
https://tlolink.com/2hwu84Y
Neuliep, James W. (2017) Chapter 2, "The Cultural Context," discusses the cultural dimensions and how they show cultural context.

[19] *Geert Hofstede's website*
https://geert-hofstede.com/
Based on his research at IBM, Geert Hofstede developed the cultural dimensions as a way of understanding the impact of culture on communication in a multicultural corporate environment.

Ethnography by Laura Di Tullio

[20] *Cultural Dimensions*
https://geert-hofstede.com/cultural-dimensions.html
Hofstede, Geert. An explanation of the cultural dimensions that Hofstede developed at IBM.

[21] *American Dreaming: Refugees from Corporate Work seek the Good Life*
https://tlolink.com/2xJfFMS
Burrow, David. (2008) How to use ethnography for in-depth consumer insight.

[22] *Intro to Discourse Communities and Ethnographic Writing*
https://www.youtube.com/watch?v=jj9gzr5y54U
LaVecchia, Christina M. (2016) Lecture on YouTube that discusses discourse communities.

[23] *Ways with Words: Language, Life, and Work in Communities and Classrooms*
https://www.amazon.com/dp/0521273196
Heath, Shirley Brice. (1999) Page 13 discusses conceptual categories of composition.

[24] *Does corporate ethnography suck? A cultural analysis of academic critiques of private-sector ethnography*
https://tlolink.com/2y6vyxL
Ladner, Sam. (2012) *Ethnography Matters* blog post that discusses the problems and challenges with corporate ethnography. There are 3 parts to the post.

[25] *Ethnographic research a key to strategy*
https://hbr.org/2009/03/ethnographic-research-a-key-to-strategy
Anderson, Ken. (March 2009) An article in *Harvard Business Review* that discusses ways a company can use ethnography to inform corporate strategy.

[26] *Lost in Translation: 8 International Marketing Fails*
https://tlolink.com/2fnV9Xq
Brooks, Chad. (2013) A *Business News Daily* blog post that describes some of the more famous marketing blunders.

Exact match by Val Swisher

[27] *SDL Help, Translation Memory Match*
https://tlolink.com/2foZE4h
Help topic that explains how SDL Worldserver determines exact and fuzzy matches.

[28] *Pricing TM Workflow*
https://tlolink.com/2yFDfIf
GALA. Blog post by Mike Karpa that discusses the evolving thinking about pricing exact matches in translation and how context affects the usefulness of an exact match.

[29] *The Fuzziness of Fuzzy Matches*
https://www.tm-town.com/blog/the-fuzziness-of-fuzzy-matches
TM-Town. Blog post that explains how matches are determined.

[30] *Fuzzy Matching in Theory and in Practice*
http://dig.multilingual.com/2007-09/index.html?page=39
MultiLingual magazine. Article by Richard Sikes that explains how matching works.

Fluency by Catherine Deschamps-Potter

[31] *Duolingo discussion about fluency vs proficiency*
https://www.duolingo.com/comment/1276332/Fluency-vs-Proficiency
Interesting perspective on fluency vs. proficiency.

[32] *What is Fluency?*
http://www.thebabeltimes.com/content/defining-fluent
Liedel, Emily. Article about what fluency in a second language means.

[33] *Choosing Your Vocabulary*
https://fluent-forever.com/the-method/vocabulary/
Wyner, Gabriel. *Fluent Forever* blog post about how to build your vocabulary in a new language.

[34] *Lexical Facts, The Economist*
https://www.economist.com/blogs/johnson/2013/05/vocabulary-size
The Economist. Johnson column that talks about fluency levels.

[35] *Test Your Vocabulary Quiz*
http://testyourvocab.com
Fun quiz that tests your English language vocabulary.

[36] *Oral Language and Vocabulary Development: Kindergarten & First Grade*
https://tlolink.com/2xK5S9d
Dahlgren, Dr. Mary E. Slide presentation that explains language development in children.

[37] *Vocabulary: Does Size Matter?*
https://tlolink.com/2fo9inJ
Duebel, D. *Edublog* post that discusses whether vocabulary size is more important than how one uses the words he or she knows.

[38] *Vocabulary Size*
https://tlolink.com/2xvJPmM
Shea, Ammon. *New York Times* article about vocabulary size and how that vocabulary gets used.

Globalization (g11n) by Anna Schlegel

[39] *Truly Global: The Theory and Practice of Bringing Your Company to International Markets*
https://www.amazon.com/dp/1460287053
Schlegel, Anna N. End-to-end mapping of what it takes for a company to go global.

[40] *Building Ad-hoc Localization Metrics into Optimized Globalization Business Intelligence*
https://tlolink.com/2y6QBQC
Burbach, Barbara. GALA webinar on collecting and aggregating metrics on localization and globalization to inform business intelligence activities. Subscription required.

Glossary by Pam Estes Brewer

[41] *The Global English Style Guide: Writing Clear, Translatable Documentation for a Global Market*
https://www.sas.com/sas/books.html
Kohl, J.R. (2008). SAS Publishing.

[42] *One company's efforts to improve translation and localization*
https://www.stc.org/techcomm/
Walmer, D. (1999). *Technical Communication*, no. 2nd Q:230-237.

[43] *International Virtual Teams: Engineering Global Success*
Brewer, Pam Estes. (2015). IEEE PCS Professional Engineering Communication Series.

Glossary of Standards Terms by Arle Lommel

[44] *Translation and Localization Industry Standards*
https://tlolink.com/2g3WsPf
GALA. List of translation and localization industry standards at GALA.

[45] *Information on the Americans with Disabilities Act*
https://www.ada.gov
US Department of Justice. Website that supports the Americans with Disabilities Act.

[46] *GSA Government-wide Section 508 Accessibility Program*
https://www.section508.gov
US General Services Administration (GSA). Resources for complying with Section 508 accessibility requirements for information technology.

[47] *Web Content Accessibility Guidelines (WCAG) 2.1*
https://www.w3.org/TR/WCAG21/
Worldwide Web Consortium (W3C). Recommendations for making web content more accessible.

[48] *Directive of the European Parliament and of the Council on the Accessibility of the Websites and Mobile Applications of Public Sector Bodies (Directive 2016/2102/EU)*
https://tlolink.com/2hBnZ7m
European Parliament. Directive to make websites and apps more accessible in the European Union.

[49] *International Commission on Technology and Accessibility (ICTA)*
http://www.riglobal.org/about/working-commissions/
Commission sponsored by Rehabilitation International Global that focuses on promoting accessibility.

[50] *Agile Manifesto*
http://agilemanifesto.org
Beck, Kent, et al. Statement of principles that formed the basis for Agile methodologies.

[51] *LISA OSCAR Standards*
https://gala-global.org/lisa-oscar-standards
GALA. Website containing references to standards previously held by Localization Industry Standards Association (LISA).

[52] *LISA QA Metric*
https://tlolink.com/2fBimcE
LISA. A quality assurance (QA) model used to help determine the quality of translations based on reviewer feedback.

[53] *Quality Translation 21 (QT21). Multidimensional Quality Metrics (MQM) Definition*
http://qt21.eu/mqm-definition
Document that defines the MQM framework.

[54] *Term Base eXchange (TBX)*
http://ttt.org/oscarstandards/tbx
LISA OSCAR. XML standard for defining languages that represent terminology.

[55] *ISO 17100:2015(en) Translation services — Requirements for translation services*
https://www.iso.org/obp/ui/#iso:std:iso:17100:ed-1:v1:en
ISO. Available for purchase from ISO.

In-Country Review (ICR) by Alison Toon

[56] *Best Practices for Client Review Processes*
https://tlolink.com/2yEC6k1
Txabarriaga, Rocio. Common Sense Advisory. Available for purchase.

[57] *Enabling Globalization: A Guide to Using Localization to Penetrate International Markets*
https://globalvis.com/resources/localization-ebook/
Chapter 12, "Selecting your In-Country Reviewers."

[58] *Why In-Country Review Is So Painful — And How You Can Fix It*
https://www.smartling.com/blog/in-country-review-painful-fix/
Smartling. (24 April 2014) Post describing best practices for in-country reviews.

Internationalization (i18n) by John Yunker

[59] *Think Outside the Country: A Guide to Going Global and Succeeding in the Translation Economy*
http://www.bytelevelbooks.com/books/thinkoutsidecountry.html
Yunker, John. Book summary for John Yunker's latest book on globalization and internationalization.

[60] *W3C Internationalization Activity*
https://www.w3.org/International/
The latest from the W3C Internationalization Committee.

Internationalization Tag Set (ITS) by Felix Sasaki

[61] *W3C site for Internationalization Tag Set*
https://www.w3.org/TR/its20/
Site provides the latest version of the standard.

Interoperability by Gábor Ugray

[62] *TMX on Wikipedia*
https://en.wikipedia.org/wiki/Translation_Memory_eXchange
Overview of TMX, the industry's most influential standard for the exchange of translation memories.

[63] *XLIFF specification*
http://docs.oasis-open.org/xliff/xliff-core/xliff-core.html
The specification of XLIFF, an indispensable file format for the exchange of bilingual content.

Interpreting by Nataly Kelly

[64] *International Association of Conference Interpreters*
https://aiic.net/
The International Association of Conference Interpreters is the only global association of conference interpreters; it brings together more than 3,000 professionals from every continent.

[65] *Found in Translation: How Translation Shapes Our Lives and Transforms the World*
https://www.amazon.com/dp/039953797X
Kelly, Nataly and Jost Zetzsche. This book provides extensive insight into many different types of interpreting and translation.

[66] *Routledge Encyclopedia of Interpreting Studies*
https://www.amazon.com/dp/0415634326
Pöchhacker, Franz (Editor). Reference guide for interpreters that provides a list of key concepts and issues in interpreting.

Language Pair by Richard Sikes

[67] *TAUS Knowledge Base*
https://www.taus.net/knowledgebase/index.php/Language_pair
TAUS is the leading organization for promotion of machine translation.

[68] *The Importance of Language Pairs in Academic and Professional Translation*
https://tlolink.com/2fp6Ltf
Stitt, Robert. *Ulatus* blog post about why language pairs are important.

[69] *About Language Pairs*
https://tlolink.com/2xvMU6k
SDL. This is from SDL's product support site.

Leverage by Patricia Doest

[70] *Lessons from Travel Companies for Supporting Global CX*
https://tlolink.com/2fozbDI
Ray, Rebecca and Hélène Pielmeier. Common Sense Advisory report on how leveraging multilingual content benefits the travel industry. Available for purchase.

[71] *Multilingual Quality and Topic-based Authoring: A Survey of Common Practice*
https://tlolink.com/2xJwFm7
Batova, Tatiana. CIDM article that discusses survey findings for how topic-based authoring improves multilingual quality.

Locale by Chris Raulf

[72] *What is International Search Engine Optimization (ISEO)*
https://tlolink.com/2hxsIHp
Raulf, Chris. Article explaining what ISEO (also known as Multilingual SEO) is and how it can be used.

[73] *Language Localization*
https://en.wikipedia.org/wiki/Language_localization
Wikipedia. Explains localization and locale.

Localization (l10n) by James V. Romano

[74] *Translation and Localization Industry Facts and Data*
https://tlolink.com/2xzCZss
Information about the localization industry, including size and growth estimates.

Localization Engineering by Bert Esselink

[75] *Localization Engineering: The Dream Job?*
https://tlolink.com/2fo14Mm
Esselink, Bert. Article in *Traducció i Tecnologies de la Informació i la Comunicació* about the job of a localization engineer. PDF format.

Localization Strategy by Andrew Lawless

[76] *A Localized Global Marketing Strategy*
http://www.brandquarterly.com/localized-global-marketing-strategy
Singh, Nitish. A *Brand Quarterly* article about the importance of localization to a global marketing strategy.

[77] *Web Analytics Your CEO Wants To Hear*
https://tlolink.com/2y5UlSu
Lawless, Andrew. LinkedIn post about why it's important to tie localization to business outcomes when talking to the C level.

[78] *How to Avoid Suffocation from Web Localization*
https://tlolink.com/2y6zO0d
Lawless, Andrew. LinkedIn post about how automation and solid processes can help to ensure scalability and consistency.

[79] *3 must-dos before going global*
https://rockant.com/3-must-dos-going-global/
Rockant Training and Consulting. Video explaining internationalization, localization, and translation, all of which are important to your localization strategy.

[80] *How Search Terms Kill Your Business - Literally*
https://tlolink.com/2fnYJRz
Lawless, Andrew. LinkedIn post that discusses the importance of terminology management and gives some examples.

[81] *Why Localization Does Not Get the Love*
https://tlolink.com/2xJhg4X
Lawless, Andrew. LinkedIn post that summarizes a Facebook Live event Andrew did with Anna Schlegel. The link to the recording is at the bottom of the post.

Machine Translation (MT) by Don DePalma

[82] *Neural MT, Sorting Fact from Fiction*
https://tlolink.com/2yF5tCP
Lommel, Arle. Common Sense Advisory article that discusses how neural machine translation fits in the language technology landscape.

[83] *How to Improve Automatic MT Quality Evaluation Metrics*
https://tlolink.com/2xJxVp8
Görög, Attila. A TAUS blog post that discusses how to improve and automate the collection of machine translation quality metrics.

Metadata by Laura Creekmore

[84] *Dublin Core Metadata Initiative*
http://dublincore.org/
The Dublin Core Metadata Initiative (DCMI) is an open organization supporting innovation in metadata design and best practices across the metadata ecology.

Monolingual by Madison Van Doren

[85] *Monolingualism in America*
https://tlolink.com/2xvzveO
Erard, Michael. A non-academic discussion of how monolingualism is
measured. *New York Times.*

[86] *Misconceptions About Multilingualism*
https://tlolink.com/2hxky1L
Serratrice, Ludovica, PhD. *LuCiD Bilingualism Policy Briefing* article describes common myths and misconceptions about multilingualism, based
on her research with UK children at the ESRC International Centre for
Language and Communicative Development. PDF format.

[87] *Monolingualism: The unmarked case*
https://tlolink.com/2y7m6dA
Ellis, Dr. Elizabeth, PhD. *Estudios de Sociolingüística* 7(2) 2006. Academic
article on the different theories of monolingualism in linguistics literature.
Ellis also explains how the stereotype that monolingualism is the norm
is perpetuated by monolingual speakers of a dominant language, such as
English. University of New England. PDF format.

Multilingual by Berry Braster

[88] *World's Languages, in 7 Maps and Charts*
https://tlolink.com/2hxtwMn
Noack, Rick and Lazaro Gamio. *Washington Post* article about language
diversity, with charts showing number of speakers in each language, most
commonly spoken languages, etc.

[89] *Ethnologue*
https://www.ethnologue.com/
Reference materials on language-related statistics. Used by many localization professionals.

[90] *Bilingualism's Best Kept Secret*
https://tlolink.com/2hxhjHz
Grosjean, François. Discusses the percentage of the world's population
that is bilingual (more than half), and some of the drivers for learning a
language.

[91] *ASD-STE100 Simplified Technical English Specification*
http://www.asd-ste100.org/
One of the most commonly used specifications for implementing controlled language processes in English.

Multilingual Search Engine Optimization (MSEO) by Richard Brooks

[92] *Google Keyword Tool*
https://adwords.google.com/home/tools/keyword-planner/
Free tool that helps you analyze your customer's search habits.

[93] *The Need for Multilingual SEO*
http://thecontentwrangler.com/2015/08/04/the-need-for-multilingual-seo/
Brooks, Richard. Blog post on *The Content Wrangler* that goes into detail about why multilingual SEO is important and provides advice on how to get started.

Multilingual Voice Over by Todd Resnick

[94] *The Importance of the Human Voice in Multilingual Content*
https://tlolink.com/2xJGXmf
MultiLingual magazine. In the June 2105 issue, Scott Abel interviewed Todd Resnick about the importance of multilingual voice over.

Native Speaker by Alan J. Porter

[95] *Defining a Native Speaker*
Davies, Alan and Elder, Catherine (eds) *Handbook of Applied Linguistics*, New York: Blackwell.

[96] *First Language*
https://en.wikipedia.org/wiki/First_language
Wikipedia. Article describes how we acquire our first language.

[97] *Who, if anyone, is a native speaker*
https://tlolink.com/2xJoMNs
Pillar, Ingrid. Article that talks about what it means to be a native speaker. PDF format.

[98] *Who Is An Ideal Native Speaker?!*
http://www.ipedr.com/vol26/16-ICLLL%202011-L00033.pdf
Saniei, Andisheh. *2011 International Conference on Language, Literature, and Linguistics.*

Post-editing by Laura Brandon

[99] *GALA: Top Resources on MT Quality and Post-Editing*
https://tlolink.com/2hwHH4a
This web page aggregates GALA-global's top recent content about MT quality and post-editing. Includes multiple videos and articles. Note that some items are member (or paid) access.

[100] *Better, Faster, and More Efficient Post-Editing*
https://tlolink.com/2yFWPUL
Rowda, Juan. GALA article describing post-editing.

Primary Market by Esther Curiel

[101] *Definition of a Buyer Persona*
https://tlolink.com/2y5VWrx
Hubspot blog post explaining buyer (customer) personas.

[102] *Global Marketing: Contemporary Theory, Practice, and Cases*
Ilan Alon, Ilan and Eugene Jaffe. Chapter 9, "Segmenting, Targeting, and Positioning for Global Markets," focuses on global market segmentation and international market selection.

[103] *A Five-Step Primer for Entering an International Market*
https://tlolink.com/2foTdxV
Young Entrepreneur Council, Forbes.

Script by Erik Vogt

[104] *The World's Writing Systems*
https://tlolink.com/2xJbxMF
Daniels, Peter T. and William Bright, eds. This book is one of the most comprehensive works on this subject.

[105] *Writing Systems of the World*
https://tlolink.com/2yFfaRW
Nakanishi, Akira. This much lighter volume is an introduction to 29 of the world's more commonly used scripts.

[106] *Omniglot*
http://www.omniglot.com
A rich on-line encyclopedia of writing systems and languages.

[107] *Ethnologue - Languages of the World*
https://www.ethnologue.com/
An authoritative reference guide to 7,099 of the world's languages.

[108] *The Unicode Consortium*
http://www.unicode.org/
One of the most comprehensive encoding standardization efforts so far.

[109] *Brave New Words: Resources*
https://bravenewwords.info/writing-systems-resources/
Kelly, Piers. Resources page on Kelly's blog that identifies resources related to writing systems.

Segment by Jamie O'Connell

[110] *Text Segmentation*
https://en.wikipedia.org/wiki/Text_segmentation
Wikipedia article that describes how segmentation works.

[111] *SRX 2.0 Standard (GALA)*
https://www.gala-global.org/srx-20-april-7-2008
Segmentation Rules eXchange (SRX) specifications

Simship by Carmen Avilés Suárez

[112] *The Business Side: The Business Why and How of Simship*
https://multilingual.com/all-articles/?art_id=1702
Asnes, Adam. *MultiLingual*, July/August 2010. Discusses business reasons
for simultaneous shipment. Subscription required.

[113] *Translation and Localization Project Management: The art of the possible*
https://benjamins.com/#catalog/books/ata.xvi/main
Dunne, Keiran and Elena. Discusses how to apply project management
tools and techniques in the increasingly complex localization environment.

[114] *Pragmatic Global Content Strategy*
https://tlolink.com/2xIYwmo
Ray, Rebecca and Don DePalma. (27 August 2016) Common Sense Advisory publication that provides practical tips on implementing a global
content strategy.

[115] *Global Content Strategy: A Primer*
https://www.amazon.com/dp/1937434400
Swisher, Val. (2014) Provides tips on how to make your global content
more accessible.

Source Language by Hans Fenstermacher

[116] *Content Strategy 101*
https://tlolink.com/2yaZ05g
O'Keefe, Sarah and Alan S. Pringle. Scriptorium. Tips on Creating Content
for Localization.

[117] *Checklist for Writing Source Text in Plain Language*
http://www.plainlanguage.gov/howto/quickreference/checklist.cfm
From the U.S. Government effort to simplify and clarify communications:
Plain language (also called Plain English) is communication your audience
(translators, too!) can understand the first time they read or hear it.

[118] *How the Volume of Source Language Affects Localization Cost*
http://www.translationdirectory.com/article1012.htm
Fenstermacher, Hans. This article goes into some detail about why writers create too much text and some techniques that can be used to minimize it and the cost of translation.

SRX by Rodolfo M. Raya

[119] *SRX 2.0 Specification*
https://www.gala-global.org/srx-20-april-7-2008

[120] *SRX 2.0 XML Schema*
https://www.gala-global.org/sites/default/files/uploads/pdfs/srx-20.xsd

[121] *SRXEditor: a free cross-platform editor of segmentation rules*
http://www.maxprograms.com/products/srxeditor.htmluse
Includes a sample file in SRX 2.0 format with a default set of segmentation rules supporting most standard cases. It also includes segmentation rules specific for 16 languages.

Target language by Fabiano Cid

[122] *Human Computer Interaction Handbook: Fundamentals, Evolving Technologies, and Emerging Applications*
Jacko, Julie A. Chapter 16, "Speech and Language Interfaces, Applications, and Technologies."

[123] *Quora Entry*
https://tlolink.com/2hxuGHV
An interesting discussion on a translator's capabilities to handle the "perfect translation" while not being a native speaker.

[124] *How to Improve Your Target Language and Why You Should Even Care*
https://tlolink.com/2fpqCc1
Tustison, Clint. Blog post on Translation Rules website.

[125] *Source Language versus Target Language Bias*
http://translationjournal.net/journal/29bias.htm
Peterson, David. Petersen is a member of the Japan Association of Translators (JAT) with a PhD from the University of Malta. In this Translation Journal article, he discusses how bias affects interpretation and translation of both the source and target language in different ways.

[126] *Content translation/Translation tools*
https://tlolink.com/2yFxuu3
Media Wiki. Extensive information on Content translation/Translation tools.

[127] *Localization Style Guides in English, Spanish, and Portuguese*
http://www.ccaps.net/vendors/style-guides/
Ccaps also offers extensive resources for customers and vendors, in particular the Ccaps Style Guide for English, Spanish, and Portuguese.

[128] *A Practical Guide to Software Localization*
https://www.amazon.com/dp/1588110060
Esselink, Bert. Although slightly outdated, this is the undisputed industry bible.

Term Extraction by Stephanie Piehl

[129] *TermCoord*
http://termcoord.eu/
The EU's website discussing terminology harmonization efforts and providing resources.

[130] *Terminology for Large Organizations*
http://www.terminorgs.net/
Terminology for Large Organizations is a consortium of terminologists who promote terminology management as an essential part of corporate identity, content development, content management, and global communications in large organizations.

Terminology Management by Rebecca Schneider

[131] *Terminology Management DOs and DON'Ts*
http://www.argostranslations.com/newsletters/newsletter_01.html
Argos Translations blog post about best practices for managing terminology.

[132] *Errors in Translated Medication Instructions*
https://tlolink.com/2z0wErc
Patient Safety blog post giving examples of problems with translations due to inconsistent terminology.

[133] *Misdiagnoses and Deaths: Why Medical Translations Must be Done by Professionals*
https://tlolink.com/2i6lhLj
Day Translations blog post that discusses medical translation errors that caused patient harm. This post shows why translations should be done by professionals and how important terminology management can be to good translation.

TMX by Christian Taube

[134] *TMX 1.4b specification*
https://www.gala-global.org/tmx-14b
Savourel, Yves and Arle Lommel.

[135] *TMX Format 1.0.*
http://xml.coverpages.org/tmxSpec971212.html
The original 1.0 specification of the TMX standard.

Transcreation by Patrick Nunes

[136] *10 Tips on Transcreation*
https://www.gala-global.org/blog/10-tips-transcreation
Väisänen, Mikko. GALA blog post about best practices for transcreation.

[137] *The Little Book of Transcreation*
https://tlolink.com/2xuUMFi
Humphrey, L., et al. A book that explains transcreation and how it is used.

[138] *Reaching New Audiences Through Transcreation*
https://tlolink.com/2xv8Q1G
Ray, Rebecca and Nataly Kelly. Common Sense Advisory report on transcreation.

[139] *A Buyer's Guide to Transcreation*
https://tlolink.com/2y5G6Nt
Safar, Libor. Moravia blog post about how to make a buying decision for transcreation.

Translation (t9n) by Lori Thicke

[140] *Research Study Finds Compelling Evidence Linking the Financial Health of Global Companies with Website Multilingualism*
https://tlolink.com/2y5Totj
Brand strength is strongly correlated to the number of languages on the website, according to Common Sense Advisory.

[141] *Can't Read, Won't Buy*
https://tlolink.com/2xKR3mV
DePalma, Donald A., et al. Common Sense Advisory found that customers are more likely to make online purchases when they are addressed in their own languages.

[142] *Global Customer Experience Increasingly Comes Down to Content—But Not Just in English*
https://tlolink.com/2yHb6AC
Customers equate positive customer experience with being addressed in their native language, according to Common Sense Advisory.

Unicode by Ken Lunde

[143] *The Unicode Standard*
http://www.unicode.org/versions/latest/
Unicode Consortium. The latest version of The Unicode Standard.

[144] *The Unicode Standard Annex #44*
http://www.unicode.org/reports/tr44/
Unicode Consortium. The documentation for the Unicode Character Database (UCD).

[145] *Unicode FAQ*
http://www.unicode.org/faq/
Unicode Consortium. The Unicode FAQ covers a wide variety of topics that benefit both users and developers.

[146] *Unicode Character Code Charts*
http://www.unicode.org/charts/
Unicode Consortium. The latest Unicode Character Code Charts.

[147] *CLDR*
http://cldr.unicode.org/
Unicode Consortium. Common Locale Data Repository.

[148] *ICU*
http://site.icu-project.org/
International Components for Unicode.

[149] *UCD*
http://www.unicode.org/Public/UCD/latest/ucd/
Unicode Consortium. The latest Unicode Character Database.

[150] *CJKV Information Processing*
https://www.amazon.com/dp/0596514476
Lunde, Ken. (2009). O'Reilly Media. Chinese, Japanese, Korean, and Vietnamese language processing.

XLIFF by David Filip

[151] *XLIFF Version 2.0*
http://docs.oasis-open.org/xliff/xliff-core/v2.0/os/xliff-core-v2.0-os.html
The current OASIS Standard, published 5th August 2014.

[152] *XLIFF Version 2.1*
http://docs.oasis-open.org/xliff/xliff-core/v2.1/xliff-core-v2.1.html
The latest version of the current dot release, backward compatible with 2.0, to be fully ratified as an OASIS Standard in 2017.

[153] *XLIFF Version 1.2*
http://docs.oasis-open.org/xliff/v1.2/os/xliff-core.html
The legacy version of the XLIFF Standard from 2008.

[154] *Bitext*
https://tlolink.com/2hxA1il
[paid access] From *Routledge Encyclopedia of Translation Technology*.
Authoritative description of bitext: how it came along and how it is important as a collaboration baseline in translation and localization. Paid access.

[155] *Using BPM to Analyze the Role of Human Translators in Bitext Management*
https://tlolink.com/2fp4JcG
Filip, David. Presentation contains up-to-date definitions of bitext and bitext management.

[156] *Multilingual: XLIFF 2.1 Open for Public Review*
https://multilingual.com/xliff-2-1-open-second-public-review/
MultiLingual magazine article explaining the benefits of XLIFF 2.1.

[157] *A Practical Guide to XLIFF 2.0*
http://xmlpress.net/publications/xliff
Schnabel, Bryan, JoAnn T. Hackos, and Rodolfo M. Raya. (2015). An introduction to the XLIFF 2.0 standard.

Contributor Index

Subject Index

A

accent mark, 130
accessibility, 138
actors, multilingual voice over, 57
ADA (Americans with Disabilities Act), 138
Agile methodology, 77, 138
AI (artificial intelligence), 58
AIIC (International Association of Conference Interpreters), 23
alignment of translation memory, 62
alphabetic writing system, 130
ambiguity in translations, 25, 90
American Society for Testing and Materials (ASTM), 140
Americans with Disabilities Act (ADA), 138
API (application programming interface), 115, 138
application programming interface (API), 115, 138
artificial intelligence (AI), 58
ASTM Committee F43, 140
ASTM International, 140
audience analysis, ethnography in, 103
audio, multilingual voice over, 56–57
augmented translation, 48–49

B

Bayesian spam filtering, 59, 138
Berners-Lee, Tim, 141
BI (business intelligence), 126
bidirectional scripts, 81
bilingual, 95
bitext, 10–11, 119, 122–123
brands
    multilingual voice over and, 57
    strength of, 45

Brandt, Willy, 55
business intelligence (BI), 126

C

case, 130
CAT (*see* computer-aided translation)
Caterpillar Fundamental English, 89
character encoding, 64–65
characters, 81, 130
character set, 65–67
Chinese, 134
CLDR (Common Locale Data Repository), 121
cloud, interoperability in, 115
CMS (content management system), 71, 138
code page, 138
Common Locale Data Repository (CLDR), 121
Common Sense Authority (CSA), 45
compliance, globalization and, 17
computational linguistics, 58
computer-aided translation (CAT), 27, 68–69, 71, 85, 119
conference interpreting, 23
content
    hosting, 55
    managing in Agile environments, 107
    quality of, 26–27
content management system (CMS), 71, 138
content strategy
    multilingual voice over and, 57
    simship and, 107
Content Translation tool (Wikipedia), 69
context, 100–101
controlled language, 88–89
corporate strategy
    globalization and, 17
    primary markets and, 104–105

M

machine translation (MT)
  described, 52–53
  natural language processing (NLP) and, 59
  quality of, 78–79
  statistical, 10
Mandela, Nelson, 45
market, 104–105
marketing
  benefits of translation in, 45
  using localization strategy in, 32–33
market research, using ethnography in, 103
markets, 126
match
  exact, 72–73, 75
  fuzzy, 74–75
matching penalty, 132
memory (*see* translation memory)
metadata, 55, 92–93
metaphors, 21
monolingual, 34–35, 95
morpheme, 133
Morse code, 65
MQM (multidimensional quality metrics), 140
MT (*see* machine translation)
multidimensional quality metrics (MQM), 140
multilingual, 36–37
  search engine optimization (MSEO), 54–55
  voice over, 56–57

N

narration, 56
National Standard Guide for Community Interpreting (NSGCIS), 140
native speakers
  hiring as translators, 38–39
  understanding target language by, 43
natural language processing (NLP), 58–59
neural machine translation (NMT), 133
new word, 75
NSGCIS, 140

O

O'Reilly and Associates, 139
OASIS, 123, 139–140
  DITA, 113, 139, 142
  DocBook, 113, 139, 142
OAXAL, 140
Okapi Framework, 140
Open Architecture for XML Authoring and Localization (OAXAL), 140
order of characters, 81
Organization for the Advancement of Structured Information Standards (*see* OASIS)
OWL (Web Ontology Languages), 142

P

pair, language, 24–25
pattern matching, 141
penalty, matching, 132
personas, 103, 105, 127
phoneme, 133
pivot language, 25, 133
Plain Language, 89
post-editing, 78–79
pricing (*see* costs of localization)
primary market, 104–105
processing, natural language (NLP), 58–59
products, meeting local regulations, 17
project management, 127
project management system, localization, 50–51
publishing, desktop (DTP), 70–71
purchases, effects of translation on, 45

Q

Quality Metric for Language Translation of Service Information (SAE J2450), 141
quality of translations
  ambiguity in, 25
  from controlled language, 89
  from machine translation (MT), 78–79
  from term extraction, 94
  improving with leverage, 26–27
  in-country reviews (ICRs) and, 19

Colophon

About the Book

This book was authored in expeDITA, a DITA-based wiki developed by Don Day. Contents were converted to DocBook, and the book was generated using the DocBook XML stylesheets with XML Press customizations and, for the print edition, the RenderX XEP formatter.

With the exception of this colophon, the index, and the advertisement at the back of the book, the interior of this book was generated directly from the wiki with no manual intervention.

About the Content Wrangler Content Strategy Book Series

The Content Wrangler Content Strategy Book Series from XML Press provides content professionals with a road map for success. Each volume provides practical advice, best practices, and lessons learned from the most knowledgeable content strategists and technical communicators in the world. Visit the companion website for more information about the series: contentstrategybooks.com.

We are always looking for ideas for new books in the series. If you have any suggestions or would like to propose a book for the series, send email to proposal@xmlpress.net.

About XML Press

XML Press (xmlpress.net) was founded in 2008 to publish content that helps technical communicators be more effective. Our publications support managers, social media practitioners, technical communicators, and content strategists and the engineers who support their efforts.

Our publications are available through most retailers, and discounted pricing is available for volume purchases for educational or promotional use. For more information, send email to orders@xmlpress.net or call us at (970) 231-3624.

The Content Wrangler Content Strategy Book Series

The Language of Content Strategy

Scott Abel and Rahel Anne Bailie

Available Now

Print: $19.95
eBook: $16.95

The Language of Content Strategy is the gateway to a language that describes the world of content strategy. With fifty-two contributors, all known for their depth of knowledge, this set of terms forms the core of an emerging profession and, as a result, helps shape the profession.

Content Audits and Inventories: A Handbook

Paula Ladenburg Land

Available Now

Print: $24.95
eBook: $19.95

Successful content strategy projects start with knowing the quantity, type, and quality of existing assets. Paula Land's new book, *Content Audits and Inventories: A Handbook*, shows you how to begin with an automated inventory, scope and plan an audit, evaluate content against business and user goals, and move forward with actionable insights.

Global Content Strategy: A Primer

Val Swisher

Available Now

Print: $19.95
eBook: $16.95

Nearly every organization must serve its customers around the world. *Global Content Strategy: A Primer* describes how to build a global content strategy that addresses analysis, planning, development, delivery, and consumption of global content that will serve customers wherever they are.

Author Experience: Bridging the gap between people and technology in content management

Rich Yagodich

Available Now

Print: $24.95
eBook: $19.95

Author Experience focuses on the challenges of managing the communication process effectively. It deals with this process from the point of view of those who create and manage content. This book will help you define and implement an author experience that improves quality and efficiency.

Enterprise Content Strategy: A Project Guide

Kevin P. Nichols

Available Now

Print: $24.95
eBook: $19.95

Kevin P. Nichols' *Enterprise Content Strategy: A Project Guide* outlines best practices for conducting and executing content strategy projects. His book is a step-by-step guide to building an enterprise content strategy for your organization.

Intelligent Content: A Primer

Ann Rockley
Charles Cooper
Scott Abel

Available Now

Print: $24.95
eBook: $19.95

Intelligent Content: A Primer introduces the concepts, benefits, and building blocks of intelligent content and gives you the information you need to bring this powerful concept into your organization and begin reaping the benefits.

XMLPress.net

CPSIA information can be obtained
at www.ICGtesting.com
Printed in the USA
FFHW011625110319
50915302-56336FF

9 781937 434588